T5-BCJ-464

THE TEACHING OF BUSINESS COMMUNICATION

THE TEACHING OF BUSINESS COMMUNICATION

EDITED BY GEORGE H. DOUGLAS

A PUBLICATION OF THE AMERICAN BUSINESS COMMUNICATION ASSOCIATION

American Business Communication Association
911 South Sixth Street
Champaign, IL 61820

First Printing May 1978
Printed in the United States of America

ISBN 0-931874-00-9

Preface

THE TEACHING OF BUSINESS COMMUNICATION in American colleges and universities takes place in many different settings and environments. Sometimes business communication is taught in schools of business, sometimes in English departments; sometimes the function is performed by departments of communication and mass media, speech, business education, and perhaps occasionally other places as well. But wherever it is taught it is obvious that interest in the subject has been on the increase in recent years. There are more people teaching business communication than ever before and there are more new people entering the profession than ever before. It is largely to these newcomers that this volume is dedicated.

The American Business Communication Association has for many years been the leading professional association for academic people who teach business communication. The association issues two quarterly publications, *The Journal of Business Communication* and *The ABCA Bulletin*. The *Journal* is devoted heavily, although not exclusively, to research findings and scholarly studies; the *Bulletin* is the association's main forum for discussion of teaching methodologies and teaching techniques. For this reason, and because in the last few years there have been so many fresh and innovative articles in our *Bulletin*, I have decided, as Editor of ABCA publications, to assemble a collection of some of the best contributions to business communication teaching that have appeared in *The ABCA Bulletin* in the period 1972-1977.

The articles in this book are new and recent and reflect current thinking and the present state of the art. We have included articles that tell people how to set up a program in business communication; we have articles on starting a course; content of curricula; methods of teaching; problems of grading. We have articles that are mainly philosophical reflections and others that are detailed how-to aids in many areas that are of concern to the business communication teacher.

One thing will be immediately obvious to anyone who dips into this collection. Business communication teachers relish teaching. They take it seriously. They are good at it. In recent years the charge has often been made that college and university teachers are not interested in matters of teaching; that teaching takes a back seat to research or scholarly interests. As editor of *The ABCA Bulletin* for the past ten years, and as a regular attender of ABCA national and regional meetings, I have long since reached the conclusion that the business communication teachers care about teaching, and in a big way. Some of the best writing and thinking in ABCA publications has been devoted to problems of teaching, which prompts me to believe that even the long-time practitioner will take a certain delight in looking through this volume.

Mainly, though, newcomers to the field who are baffled as to how to start or where to go from here will find this collection an aid and a comfort. Another concern I have always found among members of the American Business Communication Association and the contributors to our publications is a deep commitment to the sharing of knowledge. Not only do our teachers teach well, they are eager to share their feelings and experiences with their colleagues. It is that spirit of shared enthusiasm and generosity that makes this collection such a useful one.

—George H. Douglas
Editor

Table of Contents

1

The Beginning Teacher

Joel P. Bowman

How to Survive Your First Semester Teaching Business Writing without Really Trying

Many business communication teachers begin their careers not only new to teaching but also to business communication. This can make the first semester doubly difficult. All new teachers must face the problem of assuming new responsibilities for the behavior of others, and all new teachers will make mistakes when dealing with students. Those new to business communication will also make mistakes with the material. To keep mistakes to a minimum—and to maintain a good relationship with your students when you make them—practice the following techniques: be honest, be prepared, be reasonable, and be positive. The right attitude and some extra preparation will see you through.

All new teachers are created equal . . . new text, student rosters, weak knees, and nervous stomach.

But some new teachers are more equal than others. Some begin with a good background in public speaking, some have experience in leadership situations, and some have the advantage of knowing a very great deal about their subject before they begin teaching. My remarks here are addressed to those new teachers who are less equal.

I, too, began as a less equal, and I can well remember my feelings of apprehension as the time drew close for me to face my first class. I had a required college course in public speaking, but I had never had the opportunity to speak outside the classroom. I had no real leadership experience, and I knew very little about the subject I was to teach. Like most graduate assistants in business writing, I had been borrowed from another department. My B.A. is in English literature, and I had expected my assistantship to be for an introductory rhetoric course. I was a little surprised when Professor Francis Weeks asked me if

I wanted to teach business writing—I said yes because I needed the money, but I knew that I was getting in over my head. To make me even more uncomfortable as I began to prepare for my first class, I discovered that the many years I had spent in the classroom as a student were little help when it came to my new role as teacher. As an undergraduate, I had observed my instructors closely because I knew that I would eventually be teaching. But unfortunately for those of us who attempt to learn teaching by imitation, good teachers teach so effortlessly that is is difficult to observe exactly what they are doing—the external signs don't adequately reveal the internal process. And, what is even worse, I found that when I faced my first class, it wasn't easy to remember what I was trying to imitate. I had more than enough trouble remembering what it was I wanted to say and defending what I did say from the perspicacity of my sharper students.

I made mistakes. Some of my mistakes were minor: I oversimplified; I didn't know how to allocate time and spent more time on unimportant points than I should have; and in a few cases I actually gave my students incorrect information. Some mistakes of this sort are inevitable, and while you should, of course, strive to make as few as possible, in the long run your students will not be much affected by these mistakes. The mistakes that will hurt your students are errors of leadership and have nothing to do with course material. The worst mistake I made during my first semester was to berate in front of the entire class a student I had caught cheating. My public display of anger helped neither the student nor the class, and I learned the hard way that it is better to handle such incidents quietly.

Another mistake I was frequently guilty of my entire first year of teaching was to allow myself to be drawn into arguments with my students. It takes a little practice to see an argument coming, but after it happens to you once or twice, you will see that it is important for you to extricate yourself the minute you find yourself caught up in an increasingly heated circular discussion. Usually the easiest way to end such a discussion is to ask those students who are having trouble with "the problem" to see you after class. Frequently the students who were so interested in the argument during class will not have sufficient interest to remain, and if someone does stay to talk to you, he will often be more amenable to your point of view (more willing to admit that he is wrong) without an audience present. If the student is willing to continue the discussion indefinitely, give him a couple of textual references to check and set up an appointment for further discussion. If the student actually checks the references and keeps the appointment, his point of view will be well worth hearing.

I survived my mistakes. I'm still teaching business writing, and I'm enjoying it more each semester. When it comes to learning how to teach, experience is undoubtedly the best teacher. Those of us who care about teaching eventually learn to recognize and to correct our mistakes. The practical advice I offer here cannot substitute for experience; however, there are a few things you can do to reduce your level of anxiety.

BE HONEST

You might as well admit your inexperience: your students will discover it before the first week is out anyway. Be sure to explain your background and areas of special interest. If your undergraduate work has been in communications or some aspect of business administration, you will doubtless have a different approach to the course than someone whose background is in English literature. Your students have a right to know your bias. Don't try to BS your students. Students are expert BSers, and you can't fool an expert.

By being honest, you can make your inexperience work for you rather than against you. Your students won't expect a new teacher to know everything, so after you have confessed your inexperience, it will be easier for you to admit that you don't know the answer to a difficult question. Your first "I don't know" is the hard one. Write the question down and look it up later. If you can't find the answer, don't be afraid to ask one of the senior members on your staff. Your department head won't expect you to know everything until you have tenure.

Keep in mind that your class should be a learning experience for you as well as for your students—you are learning how to teach and learning more about your subject at the same time. Make your assignments work for you. Your students can help you assimilate new material if you assign short informational and oral reports judiciously. Most of your students will enjoy the opportunity to provide information they know will be useful.

BE PREPARED

The Boy Scout motto is particularly true of teaching. If you are like the typical new business writing teacher, you will be new to the field as well as new to teaching, and you will have to put forth an extra effort to prepare for your first semester. Of course, the best way to learn a subject is to teach it, so you won't really know how ill-prepared you are until after your first semester. But go ahead and do the obvious: become familar with as many textbooks as you can, read as many back issues of *The ABCA Bulletin* and *Journal* as you have time for, and review the fundamentals of grammar and usage. Once the semester is underway, take a few minutes before each class period to prepare an outline of everything you intend to accomplish. Good organization will go a long way to help make up for inexperience. If your department furnishes a syllabus, use it. After you have taught for a couple of semesters, you'll be able to free yourself from strict adherence to a syllabus and prepared notes, but until you have developed a good "feel" for the course, the syllabus and notes will ensure coherence and logical development of the course material.

BE REASONABLE

Students are people too. While teaching sometimes has the appearance of a contest between students and teacher, education is a cooperative effort. Give assignments of reasonable length, set reasonable deadlines, and accept reasonable excuses. If you have trouble deciding what is reasonable, ask someone who has been teaching a few years (your students' opinions on what is reasonable won't be accurate). Be reasonable in conducting class discussions. Encourage your students to talk by asking questions. Never embarrass a student by saying or implying that something he has said is stupid—if you look hard enough, you can find something in the most inane remark worthy of face-saving comment. If the class gets off on a tangent, don't be afraid to let the tangent proceed to a comfortable stopping place before returning to your outline.

If because of time limitations you must interrupt somebody, do it nicely. If your students feel that you are interested in their ideas, they will accept your ideas and leadership with greater alacrity. Taking a few minutes to listen to your students can save you hours in the actual presentation of the course material. When possible, illustrate your ideas with *student* examples. Each student will think that his approach to a problem is the best, and it will be easier for him to accept your criticism if you provide examples of better approaches. By using student solutions to the problems rather than your own, you also demonstrate to the class a standard of performance for students.

Be reasonable about grading too. Grading is perhaps the most difficult thing about teaching (how much credit do you give for effort?), and you will have to work out a system that satisfies you. You should be prepared to spend several hours grading your first assignments. You will probably want to read through the entire batch of papers several times before assigning letter grades. Don't despair if your students' first assignments are all worse than you had expected. Most of your students will enter the class thinking that they already know how to write, and they will approach the first couple of assignments in a haphazard manner. When they realize that they have something to learn, their work will improve.

BE POSITIVE

Positive tone improves teaching the same way it improves letters. You will find that your students will have about the same attitude toward your class as you yourself have. Negativism is almost always a defense mechanism to guard against failure—but, with honesty, a good set of notes, and a willingness to meet your students half-way, you can't go wrong . . . so cheer up, you'll survive!

Nicholas J. Pasqual

Your First Term: Minimizing the Indigestion

Since instructors come to business communication from a variety of backgrounds—literature, business, journalism, or whatever—preparing for the first term in the business communication classroom often bears an unpleasant resemblance to crisis. This article outlines a campaign for meeting that crisis: drawing on the expertise of colleagues, and on their files and those of the department, if such resources are available; saving "real world" communications; planning the term; keeping students writing frequently, but otherwise maintaining a flexible schedule; adapting tests; and asking for student feedback; all are techniques designed to minimize the indigestion a first term teaching business communication could produce.

You're a specialist in French Literature (Or Rhetoric, Or Business Administration, Or Journalism, Or Whatever).

Today, when you walked into the office, you got The News: you're teaching Business Communication this semester—for the first time.

A committee chairmanship you could endure, or sponsorship of another student organization. But teaching Business Communication? You've never studied the subject. And beyond certain vague images, circling rather darkly through your mind, of corporate boardrooms and Hidden Persuaders, you don't know much about the topic.

Your can prepare yourself for the challenge ahead, however. By drawing on your own resources and those available to you, it's possible to minimize the indigestion and maximize the pleasure and profit in the experience.

START READING

Familiarize yourself, as best you can, with the subject matter. Read as many relevant books as time and your staying power permit, and browse periodicals in the field. Ask your colleagues for suggestions . . . and expect to get far less read than you think you should.

If you find yourself horrified by Authority X's advice on a certain point, don't be surprised; see what The Competition has to say. You will find occasional differences of approach. The more you familiarize yourself with the literature, the better prepared you'll be to face your opening lecture, and the less likely you'll be to find yourself defending a view that you question.

LOOK FOR HELP

Find out what resources are available to you. If you are fortunate, you'll have a colleague or two who knows the subject and the course, and has some files of teaching materials. If you find that you're THE business communication faculty . . . console yourself with the freedom you have to develop the course as you see fit.

Be prepared to make yourself a bit of a nuisance to your more experienced colleagues: they are incomparable sources of advice—on everything from the quality of a student letter, to the quantity of writing small enough to appease your students while keeping your name respectable in the front office. Experienced instructors can be most helpful, of course—but sometimes instructors with more recent memories of the first trip through will have more useful insights.

Check the files for handouts and exercises, too. Such exercises are almost essential for explicating the mysteries of dangling modifiers or the You Viewpoint, for example—and the more you find, the less you'll need to prepare.

COUNT YOUR OWN ASSETS

Inventory your own resources. You might want to begin by discussing some aspect of the course you're familiar with. Speech teachers, for example, could open with a discussion of oral presentations while cramming the other material.

SAVE THE POSTMAN'S CONTRIBUTIONS

Start a file. Save all your "junk mail" (you may find your attitude toward it changing), and impose upon your friends to do likewise. Eye your campus correspondence critically as well. You'll find the mailman and your employer most cooperative in providing examples at which you can Point with Pride (or Indignation)—the latest Bad News from the utility company, the most recent Pleadings from your favorite charity, or some recent Bureaucratese, for example.

LAY OUT THE SEMESTER

Plan your term . . . as best you can. The more specifically you can chart your course, the happier your students are likely to be.

If you're one of those organized souls who can plot your term, period by period, before classes begin . . . I'm jealous. For me, a less structured approach is more satisfactory. I prefer to apportion the time available among the major topics, then decide as I proceed how to fill a particular period.

This also makes it easier to take up specific grammatical questions when (and if) they need stress. With one class, the Cross you bear may be parallel construction; another class may handle this concept adequately, and discussion might cause more problems than it solved.

You might like to hang this sort of flexible lesson plan from the "givens" of the schedule: enter the major vacations, drop dates, examinations and other facts you must work around on a term-at-a-glance calendar, or on monthly calendar sheets. Then plan how many writings, and what types to assign. Once you've pinpointed assignment dates, the trick is to cover the necessary background by the assignment date. You might want some unscheduled time to prevent lesson plan and reality from diverging too strikingly.

Students will appreciate written lists of readings; generally I prefer to assign due dates as topics approach, however, and I usually do not announce specific writing in advance.

A useful complement to the lesson plan—especially if your plan is the flexible sort I describe—is a "lecture diary": a one-page form for each lecture, with spaces for recording announcements, handouts, reading and writing assignments, major points discussed, and leftovers to cover next time.

It's especially useful for keeping several sections of a course parallel, and for recording whatever agreements are necessary to keep pace with the two or three students who persist in Marching to a Different Drummer. But keep the form simple—or you'll find yourself neglecting to complete it.

KEEP THE CLASS INTERESTED

Effective teaching in the business communication classroom generally follows the principles of good teaching you're already familiar with; when it differs, it's largely because of the extensive writing practice this course requires. As in any classroom, keeping your students' interest is vital.

You'll find the subject matter an ally: students have relatively little difficulty understanding the importance of persuasive presentation, for instance. This is especially so if you use illustrations familiar to your students; the latest campus hassles over housing regulations or reserved parking would do nicely.

Encourage dialogue in the classroom; lecture only when it's really necessary. You'll find students far more interested and attentive when participating regularly. This means you must learn—and use their names. If that requires the Mickey Mouse of seating charts and roll calls the first week or two, it's effort well spent.

Operate in the classroom by the principles you're pushing. Students will take your pronouncements about justifying negative news far more seriously if you justify your unpopular decisions, and they'll be far more inclined to word criticism positively if you do so.

Show lots of writing examples, both good and bad. Here your best ally is the overhead projector; it makes possible, as nothing else can, focusing a roomful of minds on the critical judgements you're attempting to develop. If an overhead is not readily available . . . consult a good source on persuasion, and prepare to practice persuasive prinicples on your chairman.

Vary the pace occasionally; even the best of techniques can be overused. Invite a visiting speaker: he (or she) will have considerably more credibility than the Hometown Prophet in stressing the importance of good writing, for example. Placement directors can be helpful speakers, or you might schedule a mock job interview. In-class writing can be an effective contrast; so can a week of individual conferences substituted for lectures.

And carry a "spare tire" with you—a transparency of a letter to critique, an exercise, or a case for in-class writing. It could be useful some day when Inspiration deserts.

KEEP THE CLASS WRITING

Have your students write frequently. And when you assign writing, prepare the way carefully. Students frequently don't understand all the implications of a situation—and frequently you may not realize, until you start grading, all the assumptions you made in assessing the case. Thus time spent clarifying your assumptions and discussing the case beforehand usually improves student solutions markedly.

Perhaps you'll also want to write a solution yourself before grading, or even before making the assignments. That way you're more familiar with the issues the case poses, and better aware of what expectations are reasonable. Be careful, however, that prewriting doesn't blind you to effective approaches that differ from yours.

Because of the cumulative nature of the material, you'll want to impress students with the importance of submitting work promptly. And because of the volume of grading, you may want to assess penalties for late papers. If so, you'll be doubly obligated to return papers promptly.

Your critiques of student writing are, of course, one of the most useful ways to teach. When you return an assignment, throw one or two good solutions on the overhead.

Make the transparency before you write on the student's paper; then you're free to discuss as much or as little as you wish, making changes on the transparency as you go. If you always mask the writer's name, even on good writing, you're free to show poor solutions as well. Try, however, to stress improvements.

Writing detailed comments on the papers takes time, but it's generally time well spent.

Assigning letter grades is always difficult, and especially so where something as personal and subjective as writing is concerned. Here you'll find the advice of others especially useful—but expect some differences of opinion, even among experienced instructors.

LEARN THE TRICKS OF TESTING

Testing always is work, but the effort can be reduced. Students like review sheets—list of terms for which they are responsible, or perhaps sample questions. The sheet also guides you in constructing the test.

In writing the exam, you'll need to be selective; time will never permit you to cover as much material as you think you should. Questions requiring short definitions make useful (if negative) incentives to encourage reading, although they take much longer to grade than their weight warrants.

Major essays and short cases require the student to integrate a variety of material, as well as to write effectively. Although they require more careful judgments from you, they're much faster to grade.

The best check on excessive exam length, by the way, is to assign specific writing times to each question, and then to weight points accordingly. This forces you to budget the parts of the test carefully, and you're much less likely to write an unreasonably long exam.

Once you've completed your draft, ask an experienced instructor's judgment.

ASK FOR STUDENT EVALUATION

At the end of the term, ask for your students' comments. While not the cure-all that some advocates suggest, instructor evaluations can be useful. A questionnaire will give some insight into the aspects of the course students especially like or object to, although their suggestions for changes will be less perceptive. You'll find students surprisingly charitable, in general, about your shortcomings.

If you're expected to use a standard questionnaire which doesn't ask the questions that interest you, write a supplement.

EXPECT TO SWEAT A LITTLE

Regardless of your best intentions, expect some uncomfortable moments. Perhaps you'll be overly dogmatic, or sit on a set of papers too long.

And when you flub, be prepared to admit it. That recalls the simple advice of a colleague, commiserating over my confession of some novice sin:

"Apologize," she advised. "Just tell them you goofed, and you're sorry."

Also be prepared to compromise occasionally. Reasonable though you know yourself to be, now and then your students will correct your illusions. If you're occasionally prepared to postpone a paper or an exam, you'll find yourself in a much better position to stand firm when necessary.

Even preparations of this sort—and your own teaching know-how—won't eliminate all the indigestion of your first semester teaching business communication . . . but they can minimize it. One of these days, then, you'll find that first semester nearly over, your mind and body nevertheless in reasonably sound shape.

You'll be surprised at how much you've learned, and how much you're enjoying yourself. You may even find yourself looking forward to a second semester!

Arax Hogroian

Business Communication: Introductory Lecture

Communication is the sine qua non of daily living. Messages, letters, telephone calls, speeches, reports, memos, brief notes scrawled on scratch pads—they are all forms of communication. Are they clear? Do they say what they mean? The skilled communicator tests for clarity of meaning and intent, removes unnecessary words, substitutes more meaningful words for weak ones, and examines the tone of his writing. This polishing process in writing is comparable to carefully removing tarnish that clouds a piece of silver until it shines beautifully. A clear, concise, thoughtfully written piece can be similarly elegant.

Communication is more than sending out messages. That is only half of the cycle. One is not really sure that he has communicated until he receives a satisfactory response. Communication is a two-way street. It's like the ping-pong ball that must be returned. It's like current traveling over an unbroken circuit—no loose wires.

TOTAL COMMUNICATION

Everywhere, and particularly in business, we want to be aware of the total image of communication. Although, generally, we seem to concentrate on the writing aspect of communication, we should not lose sight of the overall picture. Even before uttering or writing a single word, we have begun to transmit quiet messages.

For example, your manner of dress tells something about you. The way you stand or carry yourself says a little more.

The expression in your eyes communicates; if you have to resort to gestures, again you are communicating still another way. In speaking to someone over the telephone, you are sketching a picture of yourself, with the details to be filled in later. Voice quality and diction communicate. Your whole being is a communications tower constantly transmitting messages, some perhaps less tangible than others. Nevertheless, you constitute a complete network of communication every minute that you are facing an audience—a single person, a group, or a convention.

Basic to communication is the ability to express yourself exactly as you would like the person receiving the message to understand you. You need to communicate on his wave length if he is to receive the message clearly, without garbling.

CUSTOM-TAILORED COMMUNICATION

Even if, at times, "actions speak louder than words" and "one picture is worth a thousand words"—we cannot underestimate the value and power of the word. Words are the tools of communication. They are at the mercy of the craftsman. He may use them skillfully or clumsily. The finished product will tell. Is it polished? Does it reflect pride in workmanship?

Perhaps our society is suffering today from a lack of pride in workmanship and disinterest in work. There is no question that *writing is work*, and if we do not exert some effort in tailoring our words and thoughts to fit the occasion and need, we end up with a mass-produced message, or dull jargon.

There is a parallel between custom tailoring and effective communication—writing or speaking. We need to strive for custom tailoring with words so that we select our words and put them together to fit the measurements—audience, purpose, and occasion—the dimensions for the pattern of writing. Words have quality, precision, shading, and sensitivity. As a master wordsmith not only can you design the message, you can also fashion the response. Human relations is the key.

HUMAN RELATIONS IN COMMUNICATION

Human relations is the ingredient that shows understanding of one human being for another, his sensitivity to a situation.

Companies spend hundreds of thousands of dollars on advertising and improving corporate image. The basic underlying component for success in this area is public relations seasoned with human relations.

And so it is in writing. A few grains of human relations that reflect the writer's thought and consideration will bring a response in kind. A good test is: Try it out on yourself. How would you respond to the communication you are writing if you were on the receiving end? If your feathers would be ruffled by the tone or attitude, so will someone else's.

Courtesy is another ingredient which cannot afford to be missing. There is no excuse for neglect of it.

THE MELODY OF WRITING

Be natural—not flat or sharp. Nothing should be written in a letter that would sound stilted or ridiculous if it were to be spoken in conversation. The naturalness of face-to-face conversation should be preserved in writing. Flat, meaningless words should be avoided. Guard against sharpness; round off the rough edges. It is difficult to accomplish anything positive or constructive by being abrupt or curt.

Writing should flow smoothly. The progression of thoughts should be orderly and the transitions logical.

THE PERSONAL TOUCH

A letter that sounds like a form letter will never get the attention of one written in a personal style. The reader must feel that another human being is writing the letter, not a computer. In fact, the trend today is to personalize even the massproduced form letters, with the aid of the automatic typewriter. This machine is capable of producing copy that looks individually typed and includes the name of the recipient in the body of the letter.

Occasionally, in business, it is necessary to write basically the same letter to three or four different people. Even in this situation, it is refreshing for the writer to try to vary the wording, to reverse the word order within a sentence, or start with a different sentence opener. It is not difficult to express the same idea various ways. Our language is rich, and we should draw upon its wealth. There is no need to be repetitious and dull—except when repetition is used for emphasis. The little additional time and effort required to inject variety stimulates creativity and inspires the writer, a reward in itself.

JARGON

For purposes of this article it is unnecessary to list the expressions of business jargon, as these may be found in any communications textbook; however, it is sufficient to say here that jargon is dead and should be buried. Unfortunately business communications filled with jargon still circulate and do not disturb many—those who write or those who read—because jargon has a numbing effect. People are so used to it they don't react to it. That's just where the trouble lies.

Business communications need freshness, crispness, variety, strength, life, and naturalness to revive the reader. If there are any extraneous words that take up space and add nothing to meaning, remove them. Let your ideas stand out crystal clear.

Business is drowning in communications that are too wordy. Some writers have the mistaken idea that long words and lengthy passages impress. On the contrary, a well-planned, carefully-thought-out communication shows the writer's skill in achieving clarity with brevity. Each word counts and had better be read!

COMMUNICATION FORMULA

A communication should be only as long as is necessary to state the issue directly, clearly, correctly, concisely, courteously, and with human relations.

It's easy to recognize good writing but much harder to produce it; however, the first step is awareness of what constitutes effective communication. After that you are on the road to continuous improvement as skill develops with each writing experience. Just keep writing and rewriting until you communicate.

L. W. Denton

What of the Inexperienced Instructor?

Expanding enrollment in business and technical writing classes forces many inexperienced instructors into the classroom. The general frustration experienced by the inexperienced instructor can be diminished if the individual joins professional societies, surveys the literature, attends workshops for teachers, talks with professional editors and writers, acquires actual writing experience, and takes advantage of whatever departmental training programs he or she can. While more departmental training programs are developing, the ultimate responsibility, as always, lies with the individual instructor who must take the plunge, using all available sources of help.

All across this country, more and more English departments (in both two- and four-year colleges and universities) are recognizing the need for offering courses in technical and business writing. With the increased offerings, naturally enough, the staffing of those courses has become a critical problem. The purpose of this paper is to assess the position of the inexperienced instructor who is assigned to teach technical or business writing for the first time and then to suggest ways to reduce the amount of time that instructor requires to become an effective, efficient instructor.

Teaching technical or business writing for the first time is somewhat different from teaching an advanced literature course or another advanced composition course for the first time. Usually instructors for the advanced literature and advanced composition courses have ample background for the task; that is, the advanced course is something that they're prepared themselves to teach, and it's often little more than an extension of what they've taught at a basic level.

However, very few English teachers consciously have plotted their careers with the goal of teaching technical or business writing in mind. Such a "failing" is, of course, understandable since most English majors are English majors because they like literature. Most people agree that to be an effective instructor in pragmatic writing one needs some background in science, engineering, or business; he needs *actual* writing experience in business or industry; he must have a careful grasp of the principles of composition; and, most of all, he must have a sincere desire to teach business or technical writing—hopefully on a long-term basis. A person with these qualifications is the ideal. Reality, however, proves that such creatures are indeed rare and that fewer still are available on the job market at any given time.

What generally happens—and hundreds who teach business and technical writing can verify this—is that an unhappy department head, perhaps frustrated because she cannot locate a qualified instructor and/or because her budget will not allow her even to attempt to find one, is forced to "give" the course to some unfortunate, usually about two days before classes begin. Normally, the blessed recipient, having been thoroughly trained in the art of teaching literature, has neither background nor particular interest in the course. At the annual Conference on College Composition and Communication, a survey of the 40 to 50 technical writing instructors present usually reveals that none of them has ever actually taken a course in the subject. This is to say that most are "forced" into the course by circumstance—usually, again, by a department head who has little choice in the matter. A characteristic feeling among both instructors and department heads in such cases may well be: "It is more blessed to give than to receive."

Many of us were quite hopeful about the number of trained teachers which we hoped would be provided by the universities offering graduate degrees in technical communication, but most of those graduates are going into business and industry, rather than into the academic world. However, as enrollment in these programs increases, we may see a number of highly capable instructors appear on the job market.

INEXPERIENCE EQUALS FRUSTRATION

Examine now the frustration of those who must teach a subject area in which they have no background and quite possibly no interest. As they think about the situation and their desperate plight, all of the bad things they've heard about technical and business writing may come to mind. I list these not to horrify any prospective teachers but merely to be realistic and frank.

1. Some of their colleagues may still regard technical and business writing as something foreign to the English Department and belonging "over there where they emphasize practical things." Thus, in some cases, a certain degree of snobbery may exist, and a Chaucerian may rank higher than a technical writing specialist, even if both have similar degrees and qualifications, etc. The university scene is improving, however, and such snobbery is on the decline.

2. Instructors may not want to be pigeon-holed for the rest of their careers. Once they teach the course, they may well be teaching it for the rest of their lives. Many instructors have obtained certain positions simply because a department head or committee noticed on their credentials "Taught technical writing for two years."

3. They may be anxious about the tremendous papergrading load. This is not to say that grading loads are not heavy in other courses, but the percentage of cases of eyestrain and nervous disorders is considerably higher among those who teach technical and business writing than among those in other groups.

4. They may have witnessed promotions and raises passing by some instructors, primarily because most technical and business writing courses are taught at the undergraduate level. If promotions depend in part upon whether they teach graduate courses, then technical and business writing instructors may suffer, even if all of their other qualifications are comparable to those of their colleagues.

5. They *may* know that salaries are generally lower for technical writing teachers than for specialists in literature. Of course, there are many happy exceptions, and the situation is improving. In an admittedly unscientific survey I made in April, 1973, of 24 technical writing teachers, I found that salaries for specialists in literature may be $2,000 higher than those for technical writing specialists (academic rank, degrees, publications, research, etc., being equal).

Let's assume now that you have been assigned a course in technical or business writing—a field which you know little or nothing about. If we may also assume that you are reasonably conscientious and have the best interests of your students in mind, the question is not so much "*Will* you become an effective teacher?" as it is "How *long* will it take you to become effective?" Obviously the more rapidly you make the transition into the subject area, the better off your students will be—and, after all, they're the ones we're concerned about.

WAYS TO MAKE THE TRANSITION

How *can* inexperienced teachers acquaint themselves with the literature, teaching techniques, assignments, etc., as quickly as possible? Let me suggest six ways:

1. *Joining professional societies.* At most meetings one has the opportunity to learn proven techniques from experienced teachers and to discuss mutual problems with other inexperienced ones. Certainly the ABCA's national and regional conferences are beneficial. The Society for Technical Communication is most helpful for technical writing teachers. Its membership consists primarily of technical editors, writers, and publishers; educators are in a minority. Surely it helps to talk with professionals who apply what we teach in order to make their living. The annual Conference on College Composition and Communication offers much for technical writing instructors. Other professional groups do much to help the inexperienced learn the field. But more than this, they help them achieve a level of professionalism which they could not otherwise attain.

2. *Surveying the literature.* Several useful bibliographies are available. The ABCA's *Journal* and *Bulletin* recently have listed choice reading lists. The Society for Technical Communication publishes an extensive bibliography. A number of important journals are available. ABCA's *Journal* and *Bulletin* are the two which are most helpful for the business writing teacher. Also helpful is a new journal, the *Journal of Technical Writing and Communication*. Other publications occasionally devote space to these fields, but not on a continuing basis.

3. *Attending workshops for teachers.* For the first time, technical and business writing teachers are able to attend workshops designed solely for them. NCTE conducted a very successful

workshop in Philadelphia in 1974. Other organizations such as ABCA and the Conference on College Composition and Communication have conducted excellent sessions for teachers. These workshops are very positive signs that the profession is coming to grips with its own problems.

4. *Talking with a professional editor or writer.* Many technical writing teachers have never spoken to a professional technical writer or editor. Inexperienced instructors can learn more from one hour of conversation with a professional than they can from a month's worth of reading in textbooks. Inexperienced business writing teachers can find a business which will let them examine some of the reports and letters in its files and talk to its employees.

5. *Acquiring actual writing experience.* There is absolutely *no* substitute for on-the-job writing experience. One can find a part-time editing or writing job if one looks hard enough. Writing in a job situation accomplishes two things.

First, writing experience makes instructors much more confident of their own abilities. The difference between teaching composition to others and earning part or all of one's living by writing is obvious. Inexperienced teachers may always feel uncertain until they prove to themselves that they can hold a job because of their writing.

Second, they will discover much about the types of writing, the most desirable style, conspicuous problems in writing, preferred forms, etc., through acquaintance with working materials while writing.

6. *Establishing a departmental training program.* Training is the solution to the problem of inexperience, and the department in which the course is offered can be of more help than any other resource. A training program can take either of two forms:

It can be highly organized and rather formal, particularly when a number of new people are involved. Regular sessions involving an exchange between inexperienced and experienced teachers, grading sessions, the exchange of course outlines, sample papers, etc., are useful and necessary.

Or the program can be very informal, involving perhaps only one experienced person who is responsible for breaking in or helping inexperienced people and providing them the same course outlines, handouts, etc., that are used in a more formal program. But the point is: *someone is responsible* for helping those who need help.

For years many of us who teach literature have jealously guarded our teaching notes; we've refused to share our handouts and our ideas, demanding that new people work up their own material as we did. While such an attitude is undesirable, perhaps we can tolerate it since we're each competing with the others for jobs, etc. But in the case of technical and business writing, refusing to help an inexperienced person borders on academic chauvinism or worse. When the staffing problem is so critical, refusal to cooperate with each other may jeopardize the existence of all who teach practical composition.

CONCLUSIONS

The future for the inexperienced teacher now looks brighter than it did only a few years ago. Graduate training, especially in technical communication, is available for those who wish it, and sufficient publications are available for our purposes. The workshops designed for teachers are a sign of greater things to come for the profession. But most important, each department *must* be encouraged to help solve its own problems, perhaps by simply appointing one experienced teacher to assume the responsibility for breaking in new people.

In a way, the whole situation is similar to the current energy crisis. We each have an individual responsibility. However, in the case of the energy crisis, if we fail our individual responsibilities, a higher power will tell us what we must do, but in our departments, we have no higher authority, other than a dean or a president, and they probably don't care. So it's up to us.

2

Course Curricula and Content

William J. Lord et al.

Standards for Business Communication Courses

For any good product, quality is the determining factor in building a sound reputation. The same holds true for an academic discipline: Quality determines acceptance and respect. And that means quality in every course offering of that discipline, most especially in core courses. To achieve consistency (e.g., uniform quality), certain agreed-to standards must be set. These standards must then be met . . . repeatedly. In the following article, minimum standards for required Business Communication courses are presented. These are the quintessential results from years of classroom experience agreed upon by highly respected experts in the field.

These Standards govern a required, three-credit course in Business/Organizational Communication.

COURSE DESIGNATION

Basic instruction in communication is to be in an integrative and multimedia course. Preferably the course should be an upper-division offering. Major teaching emphasis may *concentrate* either on written or oral communication *(but not be exclusively one or the other)*, or on a *balance* between written and oral communication.

COURSE OBJECTIVES

Objectives to be achieved in course instruction are: 1) To make the student knowledgeable about *effective communication behavior.* 2) To teach the student to communicate more effectively through practice *and* evaluation of his/her skills improvement. 3) To sharpen the student's analytical abilities.

SUBJECT MATTER

Areas of course coverage are to include as a minimum *all* of the following: 1) Communication theory, media, and means; 2) The scientific method of inquiry; 3) Applied logic (through problem solving, evaluation, justification, data presentation and interpretation, decision making, and so on); 4) Expository techniques and strategies; 5) Psychology in communication behavior (such as motivation, reinforcement, perception and the like).

STUDENT PERFORMANCE

For the course with major emphasis on written communication, a minimum of twelve assignments are required. Adequate provision for student feedback is to be incorporated into the grading and subsequent evaluation of these assignments: Ten short and intermediate length pieces of nonroutine writing (letters, memos, proposals, problem formulations, outlines, etc.); one longer, analytical report; and one oral/visual presentation.

For the course with *major* emphasis on oral communication, a minimum of eight assignments are required. Adequate provision for student feedback is to be incorporated into the grading and subsequent evaluation of these assignments: Two oral presentation; two visual presentations; three short but rigorous writing pieces (such as letters, memos, proposals, etc.); and one moderate length research report, with team presentations of the results.

For the course with a *balanced* approach between written and oral communication, a minimum of ten assignments are required. The student work assignments should be distributed *evenly* across all activities. Adequate provision for student feedback is to be incorporated into the grading and subsequent evaluation of the assignments.

CLASSROOM SPECIFICATIONS

The classroom *facility* preferably should be a laboratory setting. Minimally, the room should be equipped with movable tables and chairs, and the instructor is to have ready access to visual/audiovisual equipment, such as—overhead transparency projector, opaque projector, videotape recorder, and slide projector.

Class *size* should not exceed 25 students per section, and the *ratio* of FTE staff-to-student enrollment should not exceed 1:100.

TEACHER QUALIFICATIONS

Minimally, *fulltime* teaching staff should hold a doctorate degree, with the ability to work in a multimedia framework. Some business experience is desirable, preferably in the area of communication. Academic training, ideally, would be in communication and organizational behavior *with work experience*, OR a *consultant background* in working with communication in an organizational setting.

University of Illinois

Course Description: Business and Administrative Communication

The Business Communications course was first offered at Illinois in 1902. As far as we know it was the first such course offered in a major university. Thomas Arkle Clark designed the first course. Then Professor of Rhetoric, Clark later left teaching to gain fame as America's first Dean of Men. The course was revised several times between 1902 and then substantially changed by the late Alta Gwinn Saunders. For a long time few changes were made, but then in the sixties the course was thoroughly revised into its present shape.

PURPOSES

1. To improve your ability to write for business and professional purposes.
2. To provide practice in solving business communication problems; in making decisions involving selection and organization of content; in choosing appropriate formats for presentation of information; and, to a limited degree, in making oral presentations to small groups.
3. To acquaint you with the body of knowledge about communication, communication theories and models, and the communication problems of business.

SCOPE

This is a broad basic course in Business Communication. Problems assigned or discussed arise from:

1. The communications of business with customers, clients, stockholders, and the public.

2. The internal flow of communication in the business organization from the upper levels of management to supervisors and workers and vice versa as well as communications resulting from staff relations within the organization.

3. The relations of the business organization with other businesses and with government.

ASSIGNMENTS

Fifteen to twenty problems or cases (depending on length and difficulty) are assigned for oral or written presentations. They are selected from a wide variety of types of business communications: memos, reports, letters, press releases, announcements, outlines, resumes, etc.

There are also reading assignments in *Readings in Business Communication* and in books and magazines in the library. These readings contribute to your understanding of communication in business and help you see your writing in a larger context. Readings also provide subjects for class discussion and questions for quizzes and hour exams.

PROCEDURES FOR HANDLING ASSIGNMENTS

Be sure to read the pages in your problem manual which discuss late work, meaning of grades, etc.

Usually the instructor requires that D and E papers be rewritten. Ordinarily rewriting does not cancel the original grade, but it does enable you to get credit for the work done. Rewriting, credit or not, is the best way to improve your writing style.

BOOKS AND SUPPLIES

Principles of Business Communication, Francis W. Weeks (PBC); *Readings in Business Communication*, Ed., Robert D. Gieselman (RBC); *Business Writing Cases and Problems*, Weeks and Hatch (Problem Manual); one package business writing folders (available in the stationery departments of the bookstores); desk dictionary for reference.

BOOKS ON RESERVE IN LIBRARY

Textbooks

Business Communication: Theory and Application, Raymond Lesikar (BCTA); *Communicating Through Letters and Reports*, Menning and Wilkinson (CTLR); *Communication for Management*, Norman Sigband (CFM).

Books of Readings

Dimensions in Communication, Ed., Campbell & Hepler (DIC); *Readings in Communication from FORTUNE*, Ed., Francis W. Weeks (RIC); *The Use and Misuse of Language*, Ed., S. I. Hayakawa (UML).

Books on Communication Theory

Persuasive Communication, Bettinghaus (PC); *Communication and Organizational Behavior*, William V. Haney (COB).

PURPOSES AND USES OF BOOKS AND READINGS

The textbook (PBC) presents as concisely as possible the major principles underlying effective business communication. It is not a "how-to-do-it" book.

Guidelines for applying the principles will be found in the Problem Manual. At the beginning of each section, you will see a "how-to-do-it" outline with an example of how it can be applied. Additional "how-to-do-it" material can be found in the textbooks listed above and others in the library.

The readings book (RBC) is designed to provide general background for the course along with examples and descriptions of how communication principles are applied in business and the professions.

IF YOU NEED A REVIEW OF ENGLISH FUNDAMENTALS

This course does not attempt to be a remedial English course, and class time is not available for a systematic review of English grammar. We do, however, try to help any student whose background in English is deficient. This is done in conference and by referral to these aids:

Harbrace College Handbook, Eighth Edition. Available in the bookstores. Useful for reference as well as for review.

English 2600. Available in the bookstores. A programmed learning book which will enable you to pick up quickly all the grammar you should have learned before enrolling in this course.

The Writing Clinic. Your instructor can give you a written request for help from the clinic which can diagnose your specific writing problems and prescribe remedial help through periodic personal consultations.

PROFICIENCY EXAMINATION

If you feel you are already knowledgeable about business communication and are a good writer, you can apply to take a proficiency examination which will give you credit for the course.

University of Illinois

General Outline and Schedule of Assignments: Business and Administrative Communication

This is a general outline that is used for the basic course in Business Communication at the University of Illinois. The outline is given to all students of this multi-sectioned course even though most instructors will make up their own specific set of readings and their own calendar of assignments. The general outline has always been a help at Illinois to new teaching assistants who need help in structuring a course of their own.

Specific readings, problems, and dates when assignments are due will be assigned by the instructor. Your instructor will also assign the dates for the two hour exams. There is no final examination.

In addition to assignments done outside of class, there is writing done in class for practice, and there are "performance tests" for grades. (A "performance test" is a problem assigned for in-class writing.)

Week 1

Subjects: Introduction to Business Communication and Communication Theory and Models of the Communication Process.

Relevant Readings: PBC Chs. 1 ,2; RIC Nos. 1, 4; RBC, 25-31, 32-37, 39-47.

Some Suggested Related Problems In Manual: 1, 2, 3, 4.

Week 2

Subject: Semantics and Business Writing.

Relevant Readings: PBC Ch. 3; RBC 1-13, 14-24, 165-173.

Some Suggested Related Problems In Manual: 6, 9, 10, 11, 74, 75.

Week 3

Subject: Communicating Business Information (Analysis of Purpose and Audience, Selection of Content).

Relevant Readings: PBC Chs. 4, 5; RBC 48-53, 108-120, 121-124; RIC Nos. 6, 8, 9, 17, 23; UML 29-40, 41-46, 70-76.

Some Suggested Related Problems In Manual: 5, 7, 8, 12, 15, 22, 19, 28, 29.

Week 4

Subject: Communicating Business Information (Patterns of Organization).

Relevant Readings: PBC Ch. 5; RIC Nos. 14, 18, 20; UML 79-90, 112-124; COB Chs. 6-8.

Some Suggested Related Problems In Manual: 16, 17, 18, 20, 23, 26, 32.

Weeks 5 & 6

Subject: Communicating Business Information: Writing Style (Sentence Construction, Word Choice, Conciseness, Jargon and its Avoidance, Transition, and Editing for Readability).

Relevant Readings: PBC Ch. 7; RIC Nos. 12, 10; DIC Selection from Sections Three and Four; RBC 65-73, 74-82, 83-95, 125-139.

Some Suggested Related Problems In Manual: 22, 23, 24, 27, 30.

Week 7

Subject: Report Writing.

Relevant Readings: PBC Ch. 6; RBC 60-64, 148-155.

Some Suggested Related Problems In Manual: 21, 25, 31, 32, 80.

Weeks 8 & 9

Subject: Applications (Data Sheets, Application Letters, Resumes, and Resume Transmittals).

Relevant Readings: PBC Ch. 8; RIC No. 28; DIC 75-86.

Some Suggested Related Problems In Manual: 67, 68, 69, 70, 71, 72, 73.

Week 10

Subject: Persuasive Communication (Establishing the "Image of the Organization, Understanding Reader's Motivations).

Relevant Readings: DIC Selections from Section Two, PC Chs. 1, 4; RIC Nos. 2, 16; RBC 54-59, 143-147.

Some Suggested Related Problems in Manual: 33, 34, 36, 40, 48.

Week 11

Subject: Persuasive Communication (Patterns of Persuasive Organization, Logic, and Use of Evidence).

Relevant Readings: PBC Ch. 9; PC Ch. 10; UML 164-168, 169-174; RIC No. 13; RBC 156-164.

Some Suggested Related Problems in Manual: 35, 37, 38, 39, 42, 45, 49, 50.

Weeks 12 & 13

Subject: Persuasive Communication: Writing Style (Sentences, Vocabulary, Adaptation to Audiences, Personalization in Individual and Mass Communication).

Relevant Readings: PBC Ch. 10; PC Chs. 6, 7; RIC No. 11; COB Ch. 12; RBC 96-107, 140-142.

Some Suggested Related Problems in Manual: 41, 43, 44, 46, 47, 51, 52, 77, 81, 82, 83.

Week 14

Subject: Negative Messages and Unreceptive Audiences (Selection of Content, Patterns of Organization, Control of Emphasis and Subordination).

Relevant Readings: PBC Ch. 11; COB Chs. 9, 10, 11, 13, 14; RBC 174-188, 189-199.

Some Suggested Related Problems in Manual: 53, 54, 56, 59, 62, 63, 65, 66, 78, 79.

Week 15

Subjects: Negative Messages (Psychology of Negative vs Positive Words and Phrases) and Overview of Course.

Relevant Readings: PBC Ch. 12; RIC Nos. 3, 21; COB Ch. 16.

Some Suggested Related Problems in Manual: 55, 57, 58, 60, 61, 64, 76, 84.

Margaret MacColl Johnson

A Syllabus for Written Communication

New concepts in sociology and psychology, and the meteoric growth of the field of public relations, have had a tremendous impact upon business communication practices. Management today is showing a sharp concern about improving its internal communications as well as its external communication relationships with the community in which it operates or which it serves.

The course concerns itself with business communication . . . in particular, written communication to establish links between individuals in a company and links with outside publics of the business firm. Today's communication techniques have been influenced by expanding technology that includes tools as simple as the electric typewriter, as complex as the computer. New concepts in the fields of sociology and psychology, and the meteoric growth of public relations, a relatively new area of communications competence, have all affected our perception of human behavior, creating more concern for the individual in his or her job environment. Thus, the skills needed by everyone, especially in a managerial or professional capacity today, are multiple, *one of the most major being clear and well presented written communication.* This skill, in itself, calls on other competencies, for example:

1. Sensitivity and responsiveness to people and to the why's of their behavior.
2. The ability to listen—and to express oneself effectively, often persuasively.

3. The ability to analyze, organize, and plan a course of action.
4. A knowledge of office organization and procedures.
5. Sensitivity to the different meanings conveyed by similar words.
6. Vocabulary competence and knowledge of the basics of grammar and spelling.

Students are involved with all of these competencies. A number of guest lecturers visit the class to point up actual problems business communication students will face as they move on into a career.

TEXT FOR THE COURSE

As a basic text we use *Contact: A Textbook in Applied Communication* by Thomas and Howard, published in 1970 by Prentice Hall. Extensive reading assignments are made in *Communication and Organizational Behavior* by William V. Haney, published in 1967 by R. D. Irwin.

EXAMINATIONS AND GRADING

We have a midterm examination and a final examination. These exams may involve letters and/or memorandums and short essay and/or multiple choice questions. They focus on writing competency.

Grades are based on scores in writing assignments (25%), midterm (25%), final (25%), and a business report (25%).

ASSIGNMENTS

We have at least 10 written assignments, predominantly of short length, such as memos, letters, reports, editing. There is a short *business report* required (5-10 pages) based on an interview students have with a representative from a local business firm or community organization. I ask that all assignments be typed. They are graded on content and communication effectiveness primarily, but major spelling and grammatical errors are also noted. Each student is invited to meet with me to discuss individual writing problems or goals.

Ross F. Figgins

A Course Outline: Employment Applications and Resumes

Unemployment! Layoffs! Cutbacks! Second Careers!

Department of Labor unemployment statistics seem anchored at 6-8 percent.

This translates into thousands of people looking for jobs daily. Obviously, those best prepared or most knowledgeable in this "sometimes skill" of job search will be more successful.

Paradoxically, considering the time and effort required preparing a person for a profession, a slender amount is devoted to placing them in that career. This is precisely why the following course was designed to aid people from a wide spectrum of educational backgrounds and experience—from high school graduates to established professionals. More than a resume writing course, it prepares students for each communication phase of a complete job search from leads, to letters of acceptance.

I. Catalog Description:

Researching the employment market, preparing a professional resume, and interviewing for employment positions. Communication models will be used, with emphasis on individual adaptation of the student's background. Two lectures, two units.

II. Required Background or Experience:

English 105, or instructor's approval.

III. Detailed Description of the Course:

A. Introduction: the goals of a course in employment applications and resumes. An organized approach to finding a professional position.

B. Research: not just any job!

1. What am I looking for?
2. Where do I find good leads?
3. Is there anyone to help me?

4. How do I find out more about a company?
5. What about employment services?
6. Should I keep a file?

Assignment: prepare an individualized employment survey and list of potential positions.

C. The Resume: What, Why, and How?
   1. What is a resume?
   2. Do I really need one?
   3. What should it include? Why?
   4. How much personal information?
   5. What about references?

Assignment: prepare a personal resume for a position.

D. The Application Letter: Individualize!
   1. Do I need a letter, too?
   2. What should it include?
   3. What makes an effective letter?
   4. When do I mention salary?

Assignment: prepare an individual application letter.

E. The Interview: What to expect.
   1. What is an interview?
   2. How should I act?
   3. Are there any special techniques?
   4. What about preparation? Practice?

Assignment: participate in a practice interview session.

F. The Follow-up: When and How.
   1. Should I follow-up an application?
   2. When is the best time? How?
   3. What about an interview follow-up?

Assignment: class discussion on simulated examples.

H. Other Situations: Related Application Problems.
   1. Are inquiry letters helpful?
   2. How do I write an inquiry letter? When?
   3. What about "blanket" mailings?
   4. What do I write to accept a job?
   5. How do I turn a job down?

Assignment: prepare an acceptance letter.

I. Conclusion: A recapitulation of communications principles as applied to the employment area, and a critical review of student accomplishments:
   1. A survey of the employment market and a list of qualified potential employers.

2. A written job application package—a personalized resume and application letter.
3. Completion of a Strong Interest Inventory—administered and evaluated by the University Counseling Center.
4. Familiarization with interviewing through actual practice session.

IV. Methods of Instruction and Evaluation:

Oral and written assignments, including an interview and various communications related to applications, will be critiqued and evaluated on a regular basis in terms of fundamentals of communication, organization, research, logic, and overall effectiveness.

V. Expected Outcomes and Goals:

A. The student should be able to study the employment potential in his field, research it, accumulate information and relevant data, and analyze that data in a logical and systematic manner.

B. The student should be able to prepare an individualized employment application.

C. The student should be able to interview for a position in a professional manner.

D. The student should be able to adapt the course material to various communication aspects of the employment situation.

VI. Minimum Student Material:

None

VII. Mimimum College Facilities:

Lecture room, audiovisual equipment: tape recorders and film projector.

VIII. Text and References:

No text will be required. The instructor will supply mimeographed models. Additional resources will include guest speakers from the Placement Office, the University Counseling Center, and recruiters from industry.

Additional Reference: *Techniques of Job Search* (Canfield Press, 1976) by Ross Figgins.

Karl M. Murphy

The Basic Technical and Business Writing Course at Georgia Tech

Many colleges have become interested in a basic technical and business writing course which will give their students the specific principles and skills needed for communicating in the business and professional world.

The course described below can be easily taught by faculty new to business-writing instruction. It gives the student the chief characteristics of both business and technical writing and some practice in applying them.

Keynotes of the course are its emphasis on the distinctive factors of this type of writing, its integration of principles and practice, and its use of material familiar to the students.

Many liberal arts schools today are confronted with the feeling of prospective students that liberal arts education is far removed from anything that will help them in their careers. Some of these schools are now searching for programs and courses that can be of practical, immediate use to the students.

The basic course in technical and business writing at Georgia Tech could easily meet such a requirement, and we receive frequent requests for further information about it. The description below is intended as an informal presentation that could easily be adapted to various needs and, an important point, to the capabilities of the faculty available. Even at Tech the specifics of the course vary according to the instructor, and to some extent the following description includes both the general ideas agreed on by the teachers of the course and the details I use in my own sections.

The course (English 3023) has no syllabus, and the text—which has been changed fairly often—is not considered important.

One reason for this is that we are fortunate in having skilled teachers—most of whom have served as writing consultants to business and government—and such persons tend to rely on their own knowledge and experience, rather than a text. Another reason is that we are teaching certain principles—easy to learn but hard to apply—and in so doing repetition of certain ideas by the teachers and practice in applying them by the students are considered of chief importance. In addition, we want, as far as possible, to give our classes the aura of a working business conference rather than an academic lecture room.

APPROACH TO THE COURSE

Schools which are offering such a course for the first time and do not have an experienced faculty would naturally—at least for a time—rely more heavily upon a carefully selected text and perhaps a syllabus. But teachers, like students, easily become interested in this kind of writing, and should soon find opportunities to put their knowledge to work and become practicing professionals.

The first few meetings are devoted to certain principles of communication which may be considered the underpinnings of the course. Though one might hope that all teachers of English are aware of these concepts, I have found that in most freshman English courses they are not emphasized—if indeed taught—and that they come to the students as new knowledge.

The student is shown that our course is not teaching "English" but communication, that written communication is only one form of many (including nonverbal methods) and not always the best form, that communication is not a single act but a process not complete until feedback is obtained, that the communicator is primarily concerned with achieving a goal and it is the audience which determines his success (or lack of it), and that rules of grammar are not natural laws but social conventions. These and similar principles, presented as a package, are seen by the student to embody a purposive, practical kind of writing he has not met in his earlier composition courses.

Since we find that our students, practiced though they may be in specific scientific subjects, have never been given an overall view of the nature of science, at least one class period is given over to the philosophy of science. The presentation emphasizes that science is best considered, not as a body of information, but as a series of techniques for obtaining verifiable knowledge. Other means of obtaining knowledge are shown (e.g., intuition, authority, and reason) and important scientific techniques are described (i.e., the controlled experiment, sampling, induction and deduction, and expert observation). The relationship of engineering (and of management) to science is then examined.

Most of our students have written more technical reports than business letters—at least for their courses—and we therefore begin with the former kind of writing. Technical report writing is taught basically by three report-writing assignments, which are preceded by a short presentation, with examples of both good and bad observance, of the main requisites of a good technical style—clarity, conciseness, and objectivity. In report-writing work the student is not permitted to use personal pronouns or subterfuges for them ("the undersigned," "this experimenter"). Although some authorities both on report writing and on general composition question this impersonal style, we have found it a good stylistic discipline for our students as well as a way of stressing the need for objectivity in research and its presentation. If the student later finds himself in a less formal writing situation, it is easy for him to revert to a personal style.

WRITING ASSIGNMENTS

The first assignment is a short paper, based on a content familiar to the student, and written without divisions or sections (so that the instructor can read a sample of the student's sustained writing style). The content is varied from term to term, but always involves material that is familiar to the student or can easily be mastered. These short reports always present a solution to a problem, but the student is not graded on the quality of his solution, but on the quality of his presentation. Examples of recent topics are: "Suggestions for Improving Student-Faculty Relationships at Georgia Tech," and "Suggestions for Improving the Parking Situation at Georgia Tech."

This short report is used to introduce the student to report writing as we want it done; before the assignment is completed, samples of earlier short reports are discussed in class, and after grading of the assignment, a review session evaluates the current crop of papers.

The topic for the larger report is also changed each term, but it is always a simulated business situation and one assignment is always given for the entire class. As an example, the report might be an internal one, in which a member of the advertising department selects a pen from among several possibilities to be used as an advertising sample. Two or three inexpensive types of pens would actually be distributed to each member of the class and used as the basis for the report. Another report topic might involve a product consultant's recommendation to a new company about a proposed new product, such as plastic paper clips (it is assumed that such clips are not on the market).

The assignment also includes a visual description of an object, tests on it, at least one survey, an analysis of the report problem, and some type of illustrative material. A specific format is given for the report and, again (to keep both the instructor and the students on their toes), is changed in some respect each quarter. A "Recommendations" section, a letter of transmittal (answering the letter of instruction, sent to each student), an introduction, and some type of summary are always required, however.

The report writing instruction is given as the student is carrying out the details of the assignment, and a part of each class period is devoted to questions that arise as the student does the required work and writes the report.

Usually the student is given a month to do the work; after two weeks he is asked to turn in a progress report, in the form of a memorandum. We ask that the students describe the actual status of their work in this memorandum and, to insure that they do, only grade this interim report Satisfactory or Unsatisfactory (S or U). A report is unsatisfactory only because poorly written; the student's progress on the report is not evaluated.

This part of our work takes approximately half the quarter; the remaining half is devoted to business writing, particularly the business letter.

This difference between technical and business writing is first delineated; the introduction of elements of personality, such as courtesy, being stressed. The currently more accepted formats of the letter are then presented, usually in one class meeting. The organization of the letter is next described, and the student is warned against such faults as the delayed introduction of the subject, ineffective or trite beginnings and endings, and the failure to have an organization reflecting the aim of the writer.

Business letter style, correctness in the business letter, and the attitude of the letter writer are next dealt with. In our own work we find the aspect of business letter practice in which the students are weakest is the concept of the "you attitude," or the reader-centered letter. Even the most sophisticated students find it hard (as indeed do many in the business and professional worlds) to get beyond the shackles of an immediate concern with their own interests and to visualize the reader of the letter as an individual also concerned with his own interests. Understanding the reader is the key to successful letters—a rule not at all understood by most business writers, whether students or practitioners.

Important types of business letters are then treated. The letter of information, the application (the entire employment process is explained), inquiries, acceptances and refusals, customer letters, and miscellaneous types are all given attention. Although the principles of the sales letter are explained, the students are not required to produce this highly specialized type.

Finally, the students are introduced to memorandums, as a popular type of communication. Some necessarily cursory treatment of dictation and methods of reproducing letters and reports (hectograph, multilith, and the like) conclude the course. A final examination tests the students' knowledge of the course by requiring them to write (or correct) letters and short reports taken from actual business or report-writing situations.

A course of this nature is, admittedly, only an introduction to a large field, but the effort is to give the students principles (and some practice) which they can later apply and perfect as professionals. Students react enthusiastically to this course, the more so after they have been out in the business world. A survey of industrial engineering graduates rates this course as the most valuable in the Tech curriculum. If this course is taught by willing, competent teachers it will always bring similar results.

Donald P. Rogers

New Directions in Teaching Business Communication

This article discusses a strategy for resolving conflicts between demands for theoretical legitimacy and practical application of business communication courses. The strategy is based on the integration of curriculum. A sample program is presented.

In the past few years I and many other teachers of Business, Professional, or Organizational Communication have been hearing two statements more and more frequently. The first statement, which I hear mostly from other faculty, department heads, provosts, and deans, in that, "If Business Communication is to remain a viable part of the University curriculum, the courses are going to have to become more theoretical, innovative, and academically sound." On the other hand, I am hearing, mostly from students and Placement Office administrators, "Business Communication courses are going to have to become more practical if they are going to serve today's increasingly career conscious students."

With conflicting demands from our colleagues to become more theoretical and from our students to become more practical, we could be building towards a case of mass professional schizophrenia. But that need not be the case. If we begin by understanding the demands being made of us as complementary rather than conflicting, we will be much closer to the innovative, integrative thinking that the future requires.

Does this mean that we must abandon our past? No. There has never been an academic field which cut itself off from its roots and survived. We can best build our future by building on our past. We can do this by broadening our own perspectives on our courses. What are we teaching in courses like letter writing, interviewing, report writing, advertising, and marketing communications? We are teaching the *theory* of communication campaigns, the *structure* of specific campaigns, and the *selection* of techniques appropriate to the specific campaigns. Our teaching focus must become ends-oriented (concentrating on the effects which decisions produce) rather than means-oriented (concentrating on the techniques that will produce effects).

In terms of courses, this means that the basic Business Communication course would become a course in Communication Campaigns drawing upon the wide, interdisciplinary study of information diffusion systems. The support courses in Business Communication would be the courses in Employment Campaigns, Marketing and Collection Campaigns, and Administrative Communications Campaigns. This approach to the Business Communication curriculum gives us both the stability of a sound, theoretically based academic focus, and the flexibility of a varied, specialized interest student appeal. Following this approach a Business Communication Curriculum might include these courses:

BUSINESS COMMUNICATION, FRESHMAN/SOPHOMORE

101 Communication Campaigns:

An introduction to Business Communication from the standpoint of the campaign. Course includes units on the purposes of communication campaigns (persuasion, information, satisfaction), the structure of campaigns (multi-phase, multi-audience, multi-media), and various types of campaigns (employment, marketing, credit, etc.). Prerequisite: none.

102 Employment Campaigns:

Course for students pursuing post college employment or graduate school admittance. Course includes units on employment research (self evaluation, identifying potential employers, sources of employment information), campaign documentation (cover letters, resume, references, follow-up letters), and interviewing (appearance, answering questions, asking questions). Prerequisite: 101.

BUSINESS COMMUNICATION, JUNIOR/SENIOR

203 Management Information Systems:
A course on the collection, analysis, and diffusion of information necessary to make decisions. Course will include units on sources of information (employees, competition, government, etc.), storage systems (tradition, manual files, computers), and diffusion techniques (reports, memoranda, conferences). Primarily for Management and Operations Research majors. Prerequisite: 101.

204 Employee Communication Campaigns:
A course on the purposes and methods of keeping employees informed. Course includes units on communication climate variables (openness, trust, credibility), types of employee information (economic education, company status, personal interest), and internal media (house organs, manuals, bulletin boards). Primarily for management and business communication majors. Prerequisite: 101.

205 Public Information Campaigns:
A course on the nature and methods of public relations. Course will include units on company positions (environment, current affairs, government regulations), specific publics (stockholders, labor unions, government agencies), and external media (annual reports, press releases, participation in community affairs). Primarily for public relations and business communication majors. Prerequisite: 101.

206 Marketing Communication Campaigns:
A course on the role of communication in the marketing process. Course includes units on customer identification (market research, surveys, polls), communication strategy (persuasion, advertising, direct mail), and sales message construction (letters, print ads, commercials, sales brochures). Primarily for marketing and business communication majors: Prerequisite: 101.

207 Customer Relations Campaigns:
A course on methods of dealing with customers on a continuing basis from inital contact through final termination. Course includes units on personal sales (sales training, making contacts, purchase incentives), sales documentation (orders, contracts, invoices), and customer service (complaints, claims and adjustments, maintenance and updates). All majors. Prerequisite: 101.

208 Credit and Collection Campaigns:
A course in procedures for granting and obtaining credit. Course will include units on seeking credit (determining credit needs, sources of credit, credit budgeting forms), granting credit (application forms, credit checks, letters of acceptance or denial), and collections policy (invoices, collection letters, collection negotiations). Primarily for accounting, finance, and business communication majors. Prerequisite: 101.

BUSINESS COMMUNICATION, GRADUATE

309 Communication Campaign Management:
An advanced course in the planning, implementing, and evaluating of communication campaigns. Course will include units on planning (definition of purpose, audience identification, media selection), directing (materials production, crisis management, time-line budgeting), and campaign evaluation (communication audits, feedback, program variance). Prerequisite: 101 or equivalent.

310 Teaching Business Communication:
A course for students intending to teach business communication in colleges, universities, or business organizations, or intending to do communication consulting. Course will include units on instructional communication (learning theories, educational technology, training programs), consulting (making contacts, problem definition, behavioral objectives), and supervised teaching. Prerequisite: Three courses in Business Communication.

Certainly, my own orientation towards Communication Theory tends to focus on the source of the message as the primary unit of analysis, but that does not mean that campaign theory is the only way for us to integrate our courses. While campaign theory has been useful to the reorganization of our graduate courses at Buffalo, we recognized that it was equally possible to focus on the receiver of the message.

A program focusing on the receiver and built around the theories of audience analysis might look like this:

101 Audience Analysis
102 The Potential Employer as an Audience
202 Information for Decision Making
203 The Employee as an Audience
204 Communicating with Stockholders and Creditors
205 Communicating with the Public
206 Audience Segmentation
207 Communicating with Customers
208 Communication and Collection
309 Theories of Audience Analysis
310 Audience Research
311 Teaching Business Communication

And a program focusing on the channel of communication built around the theories of interpersonal and mass media might look like this:

101 Media of Communication
102 Interpersonal Media
103 Mass Media
204 Letters and Memoranda
205 Reports, Stockholders' Letters, and Publications
206 Directives, Agreements, and Contracts
207 Presentations, Committees, and Conferences
208 Telephone, Telegraph, and Telecommunication
209 Closed Circuit and Commercial Television
310 Theories of Media
311 Multi-Media Communication
312 Teaching Business Communication

The point of this argument is that we, as teachers of business communication, need to develop into unique academic service departments. This requires that we develop a complete range of courses with a clear, consistent, and coherent focus derived from an intellectually sound body of knowledge. If we have anything to offer to students and university departments, we will find our value in the practicality of our courses, the traditions of our field dating back to the Babylonian tablets of commerce, and the wealth of sound knowledge we possess. My argument is that by putting this practical, tested, experience into readily available and widely accepted thoretical frameworks, we will enhance our teaching and strengthen our departments.

We will enhance our teaching because the student will be able to relate the concepts learned in business communication courses (concepts such as communication theory, campaigns, audience analysis, media, feedback, etc.) to parallel concepts taught in other courses. We will enhance the practicality of our courses by allowing students to synthesize and use the information they have gained from other courses.

We will strengthen our departments by providing teaching support to other departments and by contributing practical experience and potential empirical tests to theoretical propositions.

James P. Zappen

Description of the Advanced Business Writing Course at Western Michigan University

This little note describes a field experience in an advanced writing course.

RATIONALE

Advanced Business Writing is concerned with problems in written communication in organizational settings. It is designed for the College of Business student who elects the minor in administrative services with a concentration in business communication and for any student who anticipates a career in business, government, or the professions. Although concerned exclusively with written communication in business, Advanced Business Writing might best be described as a course in rhetorical theory and practice. Rhetoric by definiton is the study of choice in human discourse. In organizational settings, written communication is affected by a range of variables, all of them demanding decisions by skilled communicators. These decisions may include a determination of specific subject and audience or choice of channels and media, style, format, and editorial procedures.

A PROBLEMS APPROACH

Classroom exercises are problem oriented. Students will adapt selections from a variety of business reports, articles, and pamphlets, revising in each instance with particular attention to one or several problem areas. Materials for Advanced Business Writing have been provided by editors and public relations directors in government and industry. Texts include David W. Ewing's *Writing for Results* and Robert D. Gieselman's *Readings in Business Communication*, both of which explore undogmatically the problems of the specialist in written communication.

FIELD EXPERIENCE

Classroom exercises are preparatory to on-the-job experience. During the latter part of the semester, students are assigned to University departments and offices, where they address themselves to specific problems in written communication, under the supervision of heads of administrative departments. These problems differ widely in nature and scope, but all are complex, and all demand a sensitivity to the range of variables that affect written communication in organizations.

THE PAYOFF

The investment of time and energy of both students and administrative officers is great. The rewards can also be great. Students get some exposure to a variety of communication situations, including a first-hand look at some of the types of writing actually done in organizations. In some instances, the fresh perspective of the relative beginner may turn up solutions to problems overlooked by the professionals. In any case, the first-hand experience enhances both the student's competence as a specialist in written communication and his credibility with prospective employers, a decided plus for today's job-seeker.

Don Leonard

Outline of a Course in the Theory of Administrative Communication

This short outline was a handout distributed at a workshop of the Western Regional ABCA Convention Program in 1976, and was one of several outlines for courses in administrative communication discussed at that time. The course developed from this outline shows the advantages of moving from a study of the most basic level of analysis, the individual communicator, to the most involved level, where organizations communicate with each other.

I. INTERPERSONAL COMMUNICATION (about 10 days)

A model
The filter of the mind
Transactional Analysis
Listening
Nonverbal communication
Patterns of miscommunication

II. INTERPERSONAL COMMUNICATION (about 6 days)

Preconditions
Transmission and reception
Credibility
Competition and cooperation
Conflict and conflict resolution

III. INTRAORGANIZATIONAL COMMUNICATION (about 15 days)

Structural Aspects
- Upward, downward, horizontal and diagonal communication
- Formal and informal channels
- Network analysis

Administrative Concerns
- Functions of administrative communication
- Information systems
- Communications training
- Communications consulting
- Communications auditing

Other Functional Areas
- Leadership
- Motivation
- Small groups
- Committees
- Interviewing

IV. INTERORGANIZATIONAL COMMUNICATION (about 6 days)

A firm's relationship and interaction with the community and society in general, government, labor, consumers, owners, etc.

The role of the top executive.

Getting information from the outside.

Joel P. Bowman

Course Description: Persuasive Writing

The following 15-week course outline covers the essential aspects of the theory of persuasion and the techniques required to write persuasively in a variety of common business situations.

COURSE DESCRIPTION

An intensive study of persuasive communication and its written application in business. Directed practice in the application of effective techniques of writing persuasive copy in a variety of business situations, including requests, cordial contact, sales, and education and training programs.

TEXTS AND MATERIALS

Don Fabun, *Three Roads to Awareness*, 1970. (TR)
Erwin P. Bettinghaus, *Persuasive Communication*, 2nd ed., 1973. (PC)
A good dictionary.
Access to a typewriter (out-of-class assignments are to be typed).
Some 8½" x 11" white typing paper, 16- or 20-pound weight.

RECOMMENDED MATERIALS

A good handbook of English usage. (I recommend Frederick Crews, *The Random House Handbook*, 1974.)

Hovland, Janis, and Kelley, *Communication and Persuasion*, 1953.

Yeck and Maguire, *Planning and Creating Better Direct Mail*, 1961.

A thesaurus.

SCHEDULE OF ASSIGNMENTS

Week 1
Read: TR, "Motivation"; PC, pp. v-27.

Week 2
Read: TR, "Creativity"; PC, pp. 28-56.

Week 3
Read: TR, "Communications"; PC, pp. 57-76.

Week 4
Read: PC, pp. 77-96.
Submit: Persuasive requests (ditto sheet)—5% of grade.

Week 5
Read: PC, pp. 101-116.
Submit: Persuasive requests (ditto sheet)—10% of grade.

Week 6
Read: PC, pp. 117-141.
Submit: Cordial Contact (ditto sheet)—5% of grade.

Week 7
Read: PC, pp. 144-163.
Submit: Sales (ditto sheet)—10% of grade.

Week 8
Read: PC, pp. 164-216.

Week 9

Read: PC, pp. 217-246.
Submit: Mixed message (ditto sheet)— 10% of grade.

Week 10

Read: PC, pp. 248-271.

Week 11

Theory Exam—30% of grade.

Week 12

Individual topics: Subject, conception, and outline.

Weeks 13 & 14

Conferences

Week 15

Submit: Final topic—30 % of grade.

H. W. Hildebrandt et al.

Proposal for a Master of Business Administration in Business Communication

The following descriptive statement (originally the 1975 report of the ABCA Graduate Studies Committee) summarizes the ingredients needed for a suggested program of study for an MBA student concentrating in business communication. Five intellectual and practical goals undergird the proposal. Specific requirements, within the framework of the MBA program, include: 30 hours of common core business courses; 18 hours of required and elective courses in communication; and 6 hours of interdisciplinary electives within and without the business school. Stress is placed on both oral and written communication.

BACKGROUND

In 1975 the ABCA Graduate Studies Committee reported that 121 institutions offered courses in communication. A sampling of the departments offering those courses included the following:

—Speech and Journalism
—Speech and Dramatic Art
—Communication
—Speech Communication and Theatre
—Language and Literature
—Language, Literature, Speech and Theatre
—Language
—Radio, TV, and Film
—Rhetoric
—Speech, Communication and Theatre
—Broadcasting and Film
—Speech
—English Education, Speech, and Educational Theatre

—Radio-TV
—Speech and Theatre Arts

Most schools and colleges, therefore, included their communication theory and skills courses in departments of speech, literature, and theatre. Going one step further, the 1975 report identified the following schools and colleges as having graduate programs in communication, each with a particular emphasis:

—Liberal Arts
—Hygiene and Public Health
—Public Communication
—Arts and Science
—Literature, Science and the Arts
—Communication Arts
—Education
—Arts and Letters
—Fine Arts and Humanities
—Liberal Arts
—Communication and Theatre
—Communication
—Communication and Professional Studies
—Social Science and Administration
—Humanities
—Behavioral Science
—Fine and Professional Arts
—Social and Behavioral Science
—Fine Arts
—Science and the Arts
—Creative Arts and Humanities
—Graduate School

Graduate programs in communication were housed in many departments of a university.

Based on the preceding information, the 1976 Graduate Studies Committee was asked to design a program of study for the MBA with concentration in business communication. The following suggestions are a result of that effort. This proposal should be considered *descriptive*, not *prescriptive*.

PROCEDURE

The committee proceeded as follows:

1. Catalogues of graduate schools of business and other graduate schools were surveyed to determine degree require-

ments for a master's degree; hours of work; course descriptions; core requirements; residence requirements; and other statements relating to the MBA degree and other masters degrees in communication.

2. Syllabi from colleagues were collected from the fields of communication: oral, written, and organizational communication. The material provided insight into goals, directions, and behavioral modifications expected of students at the end of their communication courses.

3. Programs of technical writing institutes were reviewed to determine which stressed technical writing and oral and written communication.

4. Discussions were held with faculty in institutions with departments of communication. Observations were collected from colleagues who teach in schools of business administration. Proposals for an MBA in communication were read and discussed.

5. A draft statement was circulated among the members of the 1976 Graduate Studies Committee. Statements of reaction were received. A final statement was sent to the ABCA Board of Directors.

6. The Chairman of the Graduate Studies Committee orally presented the report and recommendations to the ABCA Board in San Diego. Comments and suggestions made by the Board were incorporated into the present statement.

7. The Chairman of the Graduate Studies Committee orally presented the report to the attendees at the 1976 ABCA Convention in San Diego. The suggestions of the members, both oral and written, were also incorporated into the present report.

ASSUMPTIONS

The committee recognized that no single program would be appropriate in all institutions of higher learning. We fully realized that preparing a program is different from implementing a program. But, the climate for business communication appears to have improved in recent years; indeed, the national outcry for better communication training has become strident.

There is a growing trend in business to form departments that are responsible for corporate communication (internal and external, employee and the public) that require persons to have a strong background in and an understanding of the behavioral complexities of information flow, persuasion, attitude change, and opinion leadership, for example.

Accepting the above, the goal of the Graduate Committee was to lay out a *proposed* program which would prepare students to assume managerial positions requiring communication or heading areas of corporate communication. The following assumptions guided committee thinking:

1. An MBA program may consist of a maximum of 60 semester hours and is a two-year program.
2. A minimum requirement for a concentration in business communication is 24 semester hours.
3. That both oral and written communication is equally important in a definition of business communication.

INTRODUCTION

The growing vital role of communication in the modern business world has created in turn a considerable demand for persons who, in addition to having a comprehensive grasp of business operations, have an advanced degree in business communication. Public and private institutions have become acutely aware of the need for more effective information handling communication systems. Many frustrations are directly traceable to the inability of both sender and receiver to cope with the technology of information handling and the systems which carry the messages.

The program leading to the degree of Master of Business Administration with a concentration in business communication has been designed to provide such professional preparation.

Through a well-balanced program emphasizing theory and skill, the graduate student can develop the necessary interpersonal skills, the handling of written and oral argument, and the knowledge and theory of group process for the effective monitoring and administration of communication in both business and nonbusiness organizations. Such a program would offer specialized training in such relevant areas as report construction, formal and informal report writing, oral and written argumentation, communication theory research, and organization theory sytems. In addition, the graduate student would be required to go beyond the core business communication courses to explore other areas of the university that are cognate to business communication.

In recent years, business communication has attracted students with undergraduate degrees from speech, English, journalism, education, public health administration, as well as students interested in technical writing. Students with undergraduate degrees in the humanities are given an opportunity to broaden their backgrounds in business, specifically in business communication. Students with a technical or a scientific undergraduate degree can apply those skills to good technical communication.

The requirements for the MBA degree with a concentration in business communication include 60 semester hours, including a minimum of 18 hours in business communication courses and 6 hours of electives. All 18 hours are to be completed in residence as a graduate student. (Waivers from the above requirements are discussed under General Requirements.)

OBJECTIVES OF THE PROGRAM

The proposed program stresses administrative communication. While organizational administration requires that its members comprehend the basic functions of management, these functions cannot be accomplished without understanding the communication channels and the skills involved in these channels. Also, an understanding of the behavioral components of the internal and external communication process, as well as using effective interpersonal skills, is necessary for running an effective enterprise.

The interdisciplinary part of the program can be met, in most instances, by taking courses already in most college curriculums.

At the conclusion of the program, students should be able to meet their career objectives in business and nonbusiness organizations.

In brief, there are five specific intellectual and practical bases on which the program in business communication is based:

1. To introduce students to the study of human behavior occurring in organizations and the role of oral, written, and nonverbal communication in the transmission of ideas.

2. To study various communication theories applicable to complex organizations, as well as to individual handling of oral and written argument.

3. To refine the skills needed in preparing formal reports, either oral or written, which satisfies a professional in the student's area of interest, and at the same time is clear and interesting to a layman.

4. To refine and develop professional writing techniques in formal and informal business communication situations.

5. To expose students to the research in business communication, and provide opportunities for individual research in business communication.

Given these general objectives, the terminal result for the student should be a demonstration of a basic understanding of communication concepts, the research on which they are based, and other concepts which support the communication propositions.

Effective completion of the preceding objectives should enable students to translate theory and principles of communication into practical application.

Finally, the student with such a foundation in the theoretical and practical should be qualified for a professional career in communication, and, at the same time, see opportunities for further research. The MBA in Business Communication is thus a professional degree.

GENERAL REQUIREMENTS

Hopefully, students interested in a concentration in business communication will have an extensive undergraduate background in such areas as English, speech, and psychology. If deficiencies in the student's undergraduate training exist, the Admissions Committee or Counselor for business communication may propose additional work to strengthen the preparation.

Approved work in cognate fields, teaching, or other professional experience may be accepted as fulfilling preparatory requirements. Those decisions can only be made by a member of the school or department concerned.

If a student's undergraduate program, either as a BBA student or as a graduate from another area of study, contains a significant number of oral or written communication courses, it is possible, either through a placement examination or through waiver, to satisfy part of the core communication requirements. Applicants judged deficient may be admitted conditionally, but must satisfy appropriate courses before graduation. Students granted a concentration certification should have a minimum of 20 hours of courses in the school.

It must be said, however, that precise course content is less of a concern of the faculty than evidence of sound scholarship and good communication ability. Thorough grounding in the fundamentals of both oral and written communication is essential.

SPECIFIC REQUIREMENTS FOR MBA CONCENTRATION IN BUSINESS COMMUNICATION

It is possible to obtain a concentration in business communication within the framework of the MBA program. The following required courses move from the general to the specific, and move from basic communication theories applicable to both the oral and written transmission of ideas.

A student may take any of the following courses by satisfying the prerequisites for each course. The concentration includes the following requirements:

1. Sample core program of a school 30 hrs.

   Analytical Foundations
   Accounting
   Human Behavior
   Information Systems and Data Processing
   Computer Programming with Business Applications

   Social and Economic Environment
   Business, the Economy and Public Policy

   Policy Integration
   Business Policy
   Seminar

   Management Applications
   Financial Management
   Marketing Management

Analysis, Planning and Control
Models for Operations Research and Management Science

Electives

2. Concentration in Business Communication
Required Courses: 12 hrs.
Communication theory and concepts (3)
Administrative communication (3)
Communication research (3)

Electives (any two courses): 6 hrs.
Seminar in business communication (3)
Argumentation: oral and written (3)
Administrative communication in public relations (3)
Administrative communication systems and change (3)

3. *Interdisciplinary Elective:* 6 hrs.
Elective courses will vary with each university the student attends; but courses are available in various departments throughout a university. The following list is not inclusive, but indicates the range of disciplines which can supplement a program in business communication.

Economics
Collective Bargaining
White Collar and Public Employee Unionism
Industrial Organization
Government and Business

Educational Leadership
Leadership-Research and Theory
Legal Aspects of Administration
Behavioral Science in Administration and Supervision I and II

Educational Media
Audiovisual Instruction
Production of Instructional Materials—Workshop I
Seminar in Instructional Materials

Educational Psychology
Technology of Instruction
Computer Applications in Education
Measurement and Evaluation

Guidance and Counseling
Introduction to Guidance and Counseling
Counseling Principles and Practices
Standardized Group Testing
Theories of Counseling

Industrial Education
Graphic Representation
Product Design
Visual Communication

Journalism
Media Workshop
Editorial Direction
Media and Government
Reporting Social Science

Linguistics
Language and Culture
Nonstandard English
Sociolinguistics
Syntax and Semantics

Management
Administrative Communication Theory and Research
Organization Theory and Systems
Seminar in Personnel Admininstration
Problems in International Management
Seminar in Administrative Policy

Marketing
Marketing Policies and Problems
Business Research

Mass Communication
Contemporary Perspective in Mass Communication Research

The Mass Communication Process: Message and Channel
The Mass Communication Process: Receiver Systems
Communication Research Design and Methods
Media and Government
International Communication
The Black Press

Political Science
Problems in Public Administration
Public Opinion
State and Local Government

Psychology
Dynamics of Human Behavior
Consumer Psychology
Workshop in the Scientific Approach to Problem Solving
Social Psychology

Social Work
Human Service Organizations
Socio-Behavior Theory and Interpersonal Relationship
Theories and Issues in Community Helping Organizational Practice

Sociology
Social Psychology
Contemporary Community Structure
Seminar in Community Behavior and Social Change

Speech and Dramatic Arts
Communication for Leaders
Mass Communication
Studies in Small Group Communication
Theories of Argument and Controversy
Theories of Persuasion
Speech Communication Theory
Discussion and Conference

SAMPLE COURSE DESCRIPTIONS

Communication Theory and Concepts. (3 hrs.)
An investigation of theories, concepts, hypotheses relating

to communication. This course is introductory in nature and attempts to integrate the various studies from speech, linguistics, English, psychology, and sociology. A conceptual framework will be used to analyze needs, diagnose problems, and recommend courses of action related to communication. Each student will prepare several communication models.

Administrative Communication. (3 hrs.)
This course stresses both theory and practice of oral and written communication in the business organization. Emphasis is placed on individual and group performance, relating this to communication theories, briefing procedures for staff and board meetings, and concepts of semantics for clarity in communication. Extensive use is made of the videotape recorder. Situations underlying functional writing as well as the special needs of business are illustrated by actual cases. Adapting style and organization is practiced through the customary business forms: memo, letter, resume, procedure summary and report.

Communication Research. (3 hrs.)
This course is designed to provide the MBA student with the rudiments of research investigation: historical, analytical, experimental. Both the oral and the written medium will serve as the areas of study, according to the specific interests of the student. Current business reports and writings will also serve as the basis for research. The student may build upon previous case work in the area of information systems.

Organizational Theory and Systems. (3 hrs.)
Emphasis is put upon such issues as governance, technology, and the application of social science to organizational struture and design. Subjects such as organizational processes, organizational change, issues, and research are part of the course.

Seminar in Business Communication. (3 hrs.)
An in-depth analysis of the variables which affect transmission of communication. Extensive time will be placed on audience analysis, and its effect upon the logical and psychological means of message transmission. Course may be repeated for credit since content and variables will change. Topics suggested include communication processes in conflict resolution; media and graphics in communication; dyadic communication; social

psychology of organizational communication and data management.

Argumentation: Oral and Written. (3hrs.)
A study of the forms of argument, analysis, evidence, and organization applicable either to listener or reader. Studies on motivation, persuasion, and argumentation will be examined. Both oral and written persuasion assignments will be used in the course.

Administrative Communication in Public Relations. (3 hrs.)
The study and analysis of the development of corporate public relations communication policies and practices as they relate to communication with external publics. Emphasis will be placed on viewing theories and principles to influence public opinion and the problems, procedures, and practices in solving public relations problems. Editing and writing of material will supplement the course.

Administrative Communication Systems and Change. (3 hrs.)
Primary emphasis on the communication process among organizational subsystems during periods of change, problem solving or crisis situation. Strategic use of communication resources and channels during change and development will be explored. The course should result in persons developing an analytical ability to bring about change in attitude and behavior modification in business settings through the use of communication.

John E. Binnion and Edward G. Thomas

A Course in Oral Communication in Business

This article is a description of a course in Oral Communication in Business that was created to serve the needs of business students—specifically, business majors who are being graduated from a college of business administration. Because there was no standard model of such a course at the time of the course construction, it was based on the needs of college graduates as observed by businessmen and women who were willing to offer assistance. The course does not contain many of the elements of a speech course as it is traditionally known. Every effort is made to assure the student of a functional application of oral communication skills to everyday business situations. And, by and large, the presentation seems to pay off.

When the planning for this course in Oral Communication in Business first began, we were determined to make the course functional rather than theoretic. Our objective: let's be certain that we give our students something that will help them on the job; let's prepare them to assume positions of leadership.

The job, then, was to find out what "Young Executives," as they are called by Walter Guzzardi, are called upon to do when they are given an assignment which involves oral (rather than written) communication skills. To answer this we used three methods of gathering data for the course content.

1. Local business and professional persons were asked for opinions.
2. The originator of the course used his own recent background as an executive in a large multinational company.
3. The literature was examined: research reports, periodical opinion, and textbook materials.

Answers, as you can imagine, were varied. There were a few answers, however, that came out of the inquiries with some consistency. Without resorting to a great deal of discussion or explanation, we can list the most important requisite qualties as the ability to:

1. talk without using too many hand gestures.
2. talk without using jargon or inane words (e.g., "you know").
3. use audio/visual aids to supplement a talk.
4. work in various types of small-group situations.
5. use one's business background in a variety of ways, and especially in integrating business skills for problem solving.
6. speak before small groups, and especially to promote the image of the firm, specifically, and business, generally.
7. interview people—for jobs, for marketing information, for personnel matters, for administrative improvement, etc.
8. perform individual research and present the findings to the appropriate company groups in a concise, coherent manner.
9. speak to subordinates and relay information to them in the appropriate manner.

Our presentation is based on the above planning, plus classroom experience in teaching the course. Included in the latter item is feedback from employed students, graduates, and "friends" of the program. In addition, our College of Business Administration Advisory Committee, made up of Cleveland corporate executives, encouraged the program from the beginning and provided assistance in a number of different areas.

Included here, but not all-inclusive, are activities in which the students participate. Some work well with Cleveland students, but might not interest those in another city or area of the country. But if one tries and does not succeed, he has the option of trying something different.

THE PROGRAM HIGHLIGHTS

With the introductory section behind us, the emphasis will now be placed on detailing certain selected elements of the course. These follow with explanations to show content and emphasis.

Informal Presentations

Early in the course, perhaps even in the first week, students will be given the opportunity to appear before the class for their first effort in this kind of oral communication. Naturally, most are nervous.

Timed Talks. Some of these practice presentations are *impromptu* (little or no preparation time) and some are *extemporaneous* (preparation time is provided, but delivery is made without notes). Areas are diversified, and not too many talks are given in any one class period because of the danger of boredom or inattention. Each member of the class makes an evaluation of the speaker, but for the first presentation no grades are recorded. Essay areas include the following:

1. Environmental Problems: Air and water pollution, slums, waste, product safety, etc.

2. Dangers to Business: Crime, over-regulation by government, and poor work attitudes are examples.

3. Esthetic Influences: Museums, "good" music and symphony orchestras, and public buildings and their architecture are possible subjects.

4. History-related Topics: Bicentennial topics were possible at this time, but history is relevant in any period.

5. Ethnic Groups: Many cities have interesting ethnic communities, and this is particularly true of the North and East of the United States. This topic is always interesting and relevant.

6. Campus Problems: Topics might include athletics, tuition increases, student government elections, cost of textbooks, or similar controversial issues.

Informal extemporaneous or impromptu talks are limited to two minutes and the student is allowed an adequate amount of time to collect and organize his thoughts. Topics have to be carefully chosen so the student will be able to talk intelligently about the subject.

Evaluation of a Speaker. Another early activity, and one which is easy to assign, involves the evaluation of a speaker. Any sort of a speaker is fair game: minister, politician, speaker at a noonday luncheon of a civic organization, or professional person at a professional meeting. In order to have common ground for discussion, however, one must prepare the students and use a standard checklist.

Because most students have not been aware of the elements connected with speaking before groups, certain evaluative factors must be discussed. These include the following.

1. Gestures. The use of hand movements and motions is important. However, the overuse of such movements tends to

detract. Emphasis is placed upon gestures, as well as foot movements, nervous detractions (jingling items in one's pocket, pacing, scratching, etc.), and similar items.

2. Delivery. Probably the most common detraction in a speaker is the continued use of the "uhhh" sound. Others include the clearing of one's throat and excessive pauses.

3. Overuse of words, phrases. Probably the most overused phrase in today's conversation is "you know." Others, just as irritating, include "o.k." and "in other words." (You can add many more to this list.)

4. Eye contact. Personal contact with the audience is important—we all know that. One of the most important of these personal relationships involves the speaker and how he looks at his audience. Eye contact refers not only to looking at the audience, but also to eye movements which range from side to side and from front to rear. Each member of the audience must believe that he is being spoken to in a personal manner.

5. Organization of materials. Obviously the talk is better if the material is organized in an orderly manner. Students are asked to take notes so they can properly evaluate this phase of the talk.

6. The audience. Of course the speaker must talk to the audience, but before he can do that he must know what sort of an audience he has. We ask the student to use the following five types of audience divisions, and to rate the speaker on how he succeeds in reaching his particular group.

A. Apathetic
B. Believing
C. Critical
D. Hostile
E. Sophisticated

As a final part of this assignment, the student is asked to give an extemporaneous talk about his subject and the speech which was evaluated. He is not only required to make the report, but he is also required to show how the performance could have been improved.

Formal Presentations

In any college of business administration there are a number of functional areas of business in which students have decided to seek a major. The most common areas are accounting, economics, finance, business education, computer information science (or electronic data processing, if you prefer that term), marketing, and management. Any one particular school may have more or fewer, or may even use different names.

Functional Area. By the time the student enrolls in this course he has decided upon his major area of business interest and has had some advanced class work in that area. In addition, he has taken a number of core courses related to business—standard functional area courses in marketing, management, accounting, economics, finance, and so forth. In other words, he has some background in business administration.

The student's assignment (and this is a major project) is to prepare an oral presentation that will use one or more of the several audio or visual devices and techniques which are available to him. In addition, he is to make this presentation on a topic related to his functional major. He has a time limitation and evaluations are made by students as well as by the teacher.

Illustrations include the discussion of a budget (accounting major), introduction of a new product (marketing major), or the evaluation of a worker's performance on the job (personnel major). The student is also required to show a relationship of his topic to one or more of the other functional areas of business—an integrative requirement.

Because time is always so important, presentations are judged in part on the basis of the time allowance. Other judging factors involve organization of materials, use of audio or visual aids, delivery, gestures (including eye contact), appearance, vocalization, and content.

Oral History of Business. One of the major presentations each student must make is based on the history of a small business located in the Cleveland area. Since we are dealing with business majors and the course is at the junior level, we feel justified in making this assignment as it builds on their previous business courses.

One aspect of the Oral History assignment is its dependence on the functional areas of business (finance, accounting, marketing, personnel, production, supervision, etc.) as a means of organizing questions and responses. We provide a list of general questions concerning these areas. Students then may add other questions which seem pertinent in a given situation.

Another aspect of the Oral History project is the taped interview. Each student identifies the owner of a small business, gets his or her cooperation, and conducts a taped interview using a portable cassette recorder. Since the class has previously discussed interviewing techniques, conducted interviews in role playing situations, and discussed questioning techniques (direct questions, mirror questions, probes, etc.), the students are required to integrate several of the skills.

After the interview is completed the student uses the tape as the basis for a written report. All of the students have had Written Business Communication previously, so this is another opportunity to practice their writing skills. What we look for in the written report is not a verbatim transcript of the interview, but a written account of the content of the interview, organized well, incorporating information about the functional area of business, and using the principles of effective writing. We look for evidence that the student has collected relevant information, analyzed it, organized it effectively, and presented it in a highly readable manner.

From the written report and the tape, the student prepares an oral presentation which concentrates on one or two of the functional areas and in which excerpts from the tape are played to illustrate points made in the talk.

The students turn in the tape of the interview along with the written report. The teacher reviews the tape to verify that the student has correctly incorporated information from the tape in the written and oral reports. Furthermore, the tape is reviewed to evaluate the student's skill as an interviewer—putting the interviewee at ease, directing the interview, using different kinds of questions to get in-depth answers, etc.

Students get a grade on the oral presentation, another on the taped interview, and a third on the written report. These three grades account for 40 percent of the final grade—the fact that this is the last major activity in the course, and that it incorporates several skills, is the justification for the relatively heavy weight placed upon it.

Conference Planning. Because one of the important oral presentation settings is the business meeting or conference, we devote several hours to conference planning techniques. Participants in a conference will get maximum benefit only if all details are carefully arranged ahead of time.

We begin with a discussion of types of business meetings and conferences—sales meetings, briefings, oral report presentations, financial presentations, parliamentary meetings, and conventions. A good, large-group brainstorming activity is to develop a list on the board of all the details which must be considered in planning each type of meeting: site, agenda, speakers, seating, meals, breaks, housing, transportation, publicity, entertainment, equipment, facilities, etc. We categorize these into two major divisions—details concerning the program and details concerning the physical arrangements.

After such a list has been developed, it is easy to see that systematic planning is needed in order to make sure that all contingencies are covered. Thus, we may decide on a modified PERT chart for depicting activities and acts, or we may develop a checklist for planning purposes, or we may simply let students offer suggestions as to how all these different activities can be visualized and managed. Students are provided with examples of checklists and other conference planning materials they may need to use later in solving conference planning problems.

Group Work. We approach group work from two standpoints: 1) as a means of discussion, case solution, and problem solving; and 2) as a means of presentation. We begin with a consideration of group interaction as it relates to the satisfaction of certain needs people have. For example, the class discusses or reviews Maslow's Hierarchy of Needs. Then we discuss how, with the exception of the physiological needs, most needs can be satisfied by group membership and participation. Safety and security needs may be provided through group insurance, health, and retirement plans; social needs are obviously met through group membership or affiliation; esteem or prestige needs may be provided through status acquired in various groups; and self-actualization may come about through dedication to some group-supported "cause." After this very broad discussion of the "group," we begin to concentrate on specific group interaction processes—especially looking at groups formed for special purposes, such as discussion and problem solving.

Discussion techniques analyzed are Brainstorming, Buzz Groups, Phillips 66, and Role Playing. Each of these techniques is explored in the class, using simple and familiar topics or situations. Follow-up discussions attempt to isolate problems which can arise with the use of each technique.

Usually, the participants will recognize that certain roles must be played in the group situation if the assigned tasks are to be accomplished. For example, a newly-formed group usually needs an "Ice Breaker"—a person who helps release whatever tension may be felt and who can provide a more relaxed atmosphere. A "Leader" must take charge and help the group set directions (goals or objectives) and get down to work. Other group members assume "Tasks Roles" (gathering, analyzing, evaluating, synthesizing, and formating information) and "Social Roles" (providing humor, encouragement, and compromise).

Group presentation techniques are then examined. Among these are:

—Panel Discussions: All group members enter into the exchange; speakers are well prepared but do not deliver prepared speeches.

—Symposia: Similar to panel discussions, but each member has a predefined topic which he or she addresses; there is no interchange among participants as there is in a panel discussion.

—Public Dialog: A discussion between two individuals—one acts as the questioner/leader and the other as the expert. In all cases a forum is provided at the end where questions or comments may be offered from the audience or from other group members in order to clarify points or expand upon areas of special interest.

Groups are then formed for the purpose of problem solving, both in-class and out-of-class. In the Winter Quarter just completed, the criterion used for group formation was suggested by class members—they compared class schedules and agreed to form groups around their free class period during the school day. Group size was limited to five. Thus we had six groups, each with five members.

Groups were given two short cases, concerning meeting room accommodations, as in-class problems. This approach allowed the groups to meet for the first time, get to know each other, and start to work together with minimum delay. It also placed them under a time constraint as they had to reach a concensus by the end of the class period.

For the out-of-class assignment, students were given a longer case problem—The American Typewriter Company. The case required each group to assume the role of a conference planning committee. The committee's responsibility is to plan a two-day national sales conference for the company. Items produced are:

—A detailed agenda for the meeting.

—A list of requirements to present to prospective host hotels and motels.

—A work plan outlining activities to be accomplished and their target dates.

In addition to presenting these three documents as evidence of the group's work, each committee was responsible for making a presentation to the class, choosing as its topic one of the interesting features of the sales meeting. For example, one group chose to discuss its Agenda. Another group described the rationale behind each topic and why the two guest speakers were chosen. And so forth.

Other features of the presentations were that some visual aid had to be used and that one of the group presentation techniques previously studied was used.

The evaluation of the group work is based on the written documents (and an accompanying cover letter) and the in-class preparation.

Other Activities

In addition to the formal and informal presentations made by the students, other oral communication topics are covered in lesser detail. The students are called upon to use information from these sessions in preparing and presenting their oral reports and, in some cases, in preparing written assignments. One such topic is described here.

Parliamentary Procedure. Some schools have an entire course devoted to parliamentary procedure. The subject is barely touched in our Oral Communication in Business, but students are made aware of the importance of the topic. Graduates do chair meetings at an early date, though: informal group sessions, committees, church functions, and formal business groups—to name but a few. They need to know fundamental rules of parliamentary procedure, and we try to give them those fundamentals.

Students need to know about *Roberts' Rules of Order Newly Revised*, but a shorter and less technical presentation is offered in our course. Just a few rules and a lot of confidence can take a person a long way as a chairman.

Equipment and Accessories

Not any student will use all of the audio or visual devices and techniques available to him at the university. However, most of them are used during the course, either as part of some demonstration or as a part of some student presentation. The major ones we use include the following:

1. 35mm Slide Projector (including combination sound/slide applications)
2. Overhead Projector
3. Flip Chart
4. Poster
5. Strip-Tease Chart
6. Build-up Chart
7. Videotape Recorder
8. Chalk Board
9. Tape Recorder
10. 16mm Film
11. Handout

The Instructional Media Service of Cleveland State University is most cooperative in assisting students in preparing materials for our courses. Professional help is available if a presentation has to have high-quality work performed. If the audio or visual part is not to be graded for artistic merit, the student usually does his own work which may lack artistic merit but still gets across the main ideas. In either case, assistance is available.

SUMMARY

At the beginning of the course the student is encouraged to put maximum effort into the preparation and oral presentation of his materials, and to place less emphasis on the art work. However, he is encouraged to remember that in business he will usually have access to professional help for art work. He is also encouraged to seek out assistance from professional firms such as the 3-M Company and Eastman Kodak, as these and other firms have publications to help one put together good programs.

Strong emphasis is placed on the idea that appearance will add to the effectiveness of the presentation. This includes the appearance of the aids to the presentations, and appearance of the person making it. So, on presentation day, the student usually stands before the class in coat and tie (if male) or dress or pant suit (if female).

As a final point, the student is encouraged to prepare himself well. Emphasis is placed on the gathering of the information, organization of the material, preparation and practice, and the presentation itself.

The final product? A student/graduate who has poise and confidence, and one who knows how to participate in decision making, and one who knows something about his leadership potential. These oral communication skills, added to a good business administration background, are a good combination which lead to improved employment possibilities and job advancement.

COURSE DESCRIPTION
BED 381—Oral Communications in Business

Required Texts: *Basic Oral Communication* by Capp (Prentice-Hall, 1971); *Speaking Well* by Reid (McGraw-Hill, 1972).

Course Objective: To help students learn to collect and organize information on business topics and present the information orally in a concise, coherent manner. Attention is also given to group problem solving processes and impromptu and extemporaneous speaking.

Course Conduct: Each individual is responsible for preparing and presenting several talks on business topics. For some of these, preparation will include the development or acquisition of visual aids for use in the presentations. Attendance is required since the class members serve as the audience for presentations and evaluation forms are completed by class members for each presentation. This is not a traditional lecture course. Participation is expected and demonstrations of various presentation techniques are used to help students develop concepts of superior and inferior approaches.

Evaluation: Evaluation is accomplished through teacher-assigned grades on oral presentations and written projects. The major emphasis is on the oral presentations. The final examination is a written problem or case which requires the student to apply problem solving and organizational skills.

Class Assignments: The syllabus will be followed as closely as possible since the timing for oral presentations is critical. The specific assignments are outlined on the syllabus.

Point Distribution for Grades:

Book review/other oral presentation	10
Speech evaluation	10
Group project	10
Formal oral report	30
Oral history of business report	40
Total	100

Week 1

Topics: Introduction to the course. Introduction to presentation techniques. Learning to evaluate speakers.

Assignments: Preparation of short practice talks.

Week 2

Topics: Practice talks before TV (videotape) cameras. Practice in speaker evaluation. Planning oral presentations. Explanation of book review and oral history of business talks.

Assignments: Preparation of oral book review. Preparation of oral history of business talk.

Week 3

Topics: Forming groups. Group discussion and presentation techniques. Group problem solving. Interview techniques for oral history reports.

Week 4

Topics: The business conference—planning, conducting, and evaluating. Case problem on conference planning. In-class business conference case problem.

Assignments: Group preparation written and oral report on business conference case.

Week 5

Topics: Group presentations on conference case. Discussion of the formal oral report: choosing a topic, writing report text, making audiovisual aids, presenting talk. Readability scales and their applicability to oral communications.

Assignments: Preparation of formal oral reports.

Week 6

Topics: Parliamentary procedure. Chairing a meeting; oral book reviews.

Assignments: Impromptu and extemporaneous talks.

Week 7

Topics: Oral book reviews and formal oral report presentations.

Week 8

Topics: Formal oral report presentations.
Assignments: Impromptu and extemporaneous talks.

Week 9

Topics: Job interview techniques. Videotape of job interview. Guest speaker. Role playing.

Week 10

Topics: Oral history of business talk.

Week 11

Topics: Oral history of business talk. Course evaluation.

Week 12

Topics: Final examination

3

Teaching Methods and Techniques

Jean Dickey

A Contract Plan for Teaching Business Communications

The author shares a contract approach to classroom management for a "Business Correspondence and Reports" class. A contract is presented to each student with the requirements for each grade level. Both the student and the teacher, by placing their signatures on the contract, have made an agreement that if the student fulfills the contract, he will receive the contracted grade, unless he defaults. This gives the student a greater responsibility for his own achievement and also a greater degree of freedom in defining his goals than that of the traditional classroom approach.

Perhaps many of the readers will identify with the persistent dilemma which I, as a teacher of communications, have never fully resolved. The dilemma has been "How do I ever get all of the assignments graded and give the necessary feedback to my students?" Early in my own teaching career I resolved that if I asked a student to do an assignment and hand it in, I had an obligation to look at the assignment and give him some kind of feedback (reinforcement).

Through a series of events I found myself assigned as a teacher in a sophomore level course (required of all business students) called "Business Correspondence and Reports" at a time, a few years back, when enrollments were rapidly increasing and teachers were in short supply. The result was that every available space in the classroom was filled, and I became increasingly frustrated as the mountain of paper work began to push in upon both my physical prowess and mental capacity. I considered many solutions to my dilemma such as becoming a foreign missionary, blackmailing my department head so that I would never again have to teach a section of Business Correspondence and Reports, flunking 80 percent of the class so I would become a very unpopular instructor, but none of these seemed to be a viable alternative. I shared this dilemma with one of my colleagues who is an educational psychologist. He asked me if I had ever considered a grade contract plan, and then proceeded to outline some of its advantages and explain how the contract could be implemented. The next time that the hurtful, heinous assignment rolled around, I decided to execute the contract.

In a typical classroom structure in college a high degree of homogenity of student aptitude, abilities, and needs is assumed. This dogmatic assertion is based on the facts that students hear the same lecture, do the same assignments, and take the same tests. The grades are competitively assigned on some arbitrary scale or by a scheme which compares the students one to another. The first flaw in the logic of such an organization is that students are anything but alike. I find that they come with widely varying degrees of writing skill. Perhaps more important is the level of motivation on the part of each student. This motivation, of course, is a direct result of some felt need. When one includes those students who work primarily for a grade, we find that there are a few who look upon the course only as some "mickey-mouse" requirement and who are quite willing to take a "D" grade just to get the whole thing over; there are others that are aware of the continuing need for effective communication in the business community. The grade contract has been my answer to the problem of meeting these diverse needs. In short, the contract places on the student the responsibility for setting his or her own goals and executing them.

THE CONTRACT

I have found that the contract idea is so novel to the typical student that it becomes necessary to explain and answer questions about the philosophy underlying contract grading and how the procedure actually works. At the beginning of each semester I distribute to each student two copies of a grade contract form, which I revise each semester. A facsimile of one of these contracts is shown on page 90.

I explain to the students that the primary purpose of the grade contract is to give them the freedom to learn. By this I mean that I am required to operate in a manner consistent with University regulations so that I do not have the prerogative to define freedom as "total license." However, it is possible to permit the students some selection both in choice of learning objectives and level of achievement.

In the past, students were not permitted to change their contracts during the semester to a higher grade level, but if they were not living up to their original contract, to be responsible students they were to contract to the proper lower grade level. However, I plan in the future, as a result of a student suggestion, to permit a student to raise his contract at midterm to a higher level, provided he has met those requirements. He may contract down at any point during the semester.

The contract may seem to be a radical idea to some people who have come to believe that the only legitimate way to evaluate student performance is through a test. I find that some people who have written about contract grading (Dennis A. Warner and Toshio Akamine, "Student Reactions to College Grade Contracts," *The Educational Forum*, Vol. 36, March, 1972, 389-391.) have required examinations as a part of the contract. As the "proof of the pudding is in the eating," the proof of a student's performance is his ability to organize his thinking in a logical pattern and to communicate effectively verbally or on the written page. Therefore I do not require examinations unless a student has acquired excessive absences and has thus been deprived of the learning activities performed in class. (See Grade Contract on page 90.)

Students usually need an explanation of the phrase "term-end statement" as used on the contract. The following term-end statement submitted by a student will clarify this.

> On February 21, 1972, a Business Correspondence and Reports Contract for a grade of A was signed by Mrs. Jean Dickey and Me. To fulfill this contract and thus receive a semester grade of A, it was necessary to complete the requirements of the C level, the B level, and the A level contracts. I feel I have fulfilled these requirements and should receive as my semester grade an A.
>
> At the C level, I feel I have contributed positively to the small group activities, handed in written assignments when due, and met the basic requirements of the course. I have read the assigned material and am now writing a term-end statement to be handed in.
>
> At the B level, I have made an oral report on "How to Make Employee Publications Pay-Off," including an outline for this report,

CONTRACT
BUSINESS CORRESPONDENCE AND REPORTS

During the semester I would like to work for a grade of ______. I will complete the requirements stated below for this grade; if I fail to meet the requirements, I will contract down.

Proposed by ______________________________ Date ______________
Approved by ______________________________ Date ______________

C LEVEL

1. I will read the assigned material.
2. I will meet the basic requirements of the course, performing at a satisfactory level, and hand in written assignments when due. I will rewrite any work that the instructor deems unsatisfactory and return it within one week.
3. I will make a positive contribution to the small group activities.
4. I will take a final exam, performing at a satsifactory level, if my absences are excessive.
5. I will write and hand in a term-end statement, placing it in a folder along with all course assignments which the instructor returned during the semester.

B LEVEL

1. I will complete all requirements for the "C" level.
2. I will make an oral report on ______________________________
   ____
   (Some phase of communication which meets intructor's approval)
3. I will interview a business executive on communication in his firm and write a report on the interview.
   Name and/or title of person ______________________________
   Name of business firm ______________________________
4. I will perform at this level. (Most papers will be satisfactory when turned in the first time.)

A LEVEL

1. I will complete all requirements for the "B" level.
2. I will write a formal report.
3. I will work at this level throughout the semester. (Seldom, if ever, should an assignment have to be rewritten.)

and have made an interview with a business executive. This interview was with several managers of the Safeco Insurance Company of St. Louis, Missouri, A report of the interview was made and turned in.

At the A level, I have written a formal report entitled "Profile of Top Executives for American Association of Manufacturers." I feel that I have justly completed the requirements of the C and B level contracts and have worked at an A level throughout the semester.

For the reasons stated above, I feel I have earned a grade of A for the Spring Semester, 1972, Business Correspondence and Reports.

TEACHER AND STUDENT REACTIONS TO THE CONTRACT

I started this article with an honest statement of why I orginally came to try the grade contract—I wanted to decrease the paper grading chore. I have found that to some extent the contract has done this; however, much more important, the paper-grading chore is less a burden now because I have come to infer a much greater degree of ego involvement on the part of students in the written work which they submit. Their work therefore is more interesting to read. No longer do I labor over putting a fair grade on each paper. I merely ask the student to redo an unsatisfactory assignment. His goal is no longer grade but quality oriented.

The contract has caused me to question certain "sacred cows" in connection with the typical university teaching model. Almost imperceptibly I have drawn into sharper focus some of my own philosophical notions concerning the teaching-learning process.

In general, the contract has been positively received by the students. In each section there are one or two students who say that they prefer the old teacher-assigned, teacher-made tests approach. After fourteen or fifteen years in school, they had become so conditioned to the traditional approach that they needed the threat of examinations to motivate them. However, I was surprised and pleased at the candidness of students who have told me that they agreed with the philosophy underlying the contract system. Let me share with you a few randomly selected comments from evaluation forms handed in by the students at the end of the course.

1. To a great extent, the responsibility under the contract plan is placed entirely upon the shoulders of the class members,

which should be a regular part of any learning experience. One can only guess at the future probabilities that this assumption of obligation will have later on in the person's business career.

2. In other methods the student does not have the responsibility that he has under the contract plan. College should teach more responsibility, not treat you like a high school student.

3. Not all students can handle the added responsibility.

4. I thought it was fair. However, it really hurts when you see your grade fall because of your own lack of effort. Then you cannot blame the teacher for it. The contract is a good idea.

5. The contract could include an option for taking tests in place of assigned papers. Some students would be able to better themselves with this method.

6. The small group activities enhance the appeal of this course to me. They serve as catalysts in breaking down the barriers in communication between one student and another. All other classrooms that I have ever attended seem to build up the resistance to talk in the class or to talk even among students themselves . . . This class has allowed me the privilege to air my views on certain matters, and for that alone I am sincerely grateful.

7. I felt I actually learned something rather than just memorizing answers for a test. I also worked harder and was more apt to keep up. There was no cramming for tests. The competition is not among the rest of the class but within yourself.

SUMMARY OF THE ADVANTAGES OF THE CONTRACT

The phrase "grade contract" seems to be very much like Humpty Dumpty's famous expression, "When I use a word, it means exactly what I choose it to mean—no more and no less." I have attempted to communicate some things that I have learned as a result of using contract grading in a specific situation. As I view it, the grade contract has these advantages:

1. It gives a much greater degree of latitude in student assignments.
2. It helps me to be more positive in my criticism of students' work since I do not have to grade each item.
3. It appears to give to the student a choice concerning this level of achievement and the responsibility for that choice.
4. Perhaps, more important, the contract has forced me to see the individual student as a unique person.

Charlotte A. Williams

An Experimental Instructional Approach Using the Small Group Concept

---

This article describes an experimental small-group approach to teaching business communication by involving the students more intensively in the teaching/learning process. In groups of five or six, students prepared and presented material on a sub-unit of course material, prepared an appropriate case problem, and evaluated classmates' written solutions while classmates evaluated the groups' efforts in turn. In addition, all students based their report-writing project on their experiences in the groups. The preponderance of favorable attitudes expressed in course evaluations indicates that the approach has strong potential as a teaching method which engages student interest and provides integrative learning experiences.

In a continuing effort to increase the potential for integrated learning experiences in a course in written communication in business, an approach was utilized which was based on the small group concept. This course as taught at the Florida State University College of Business is an upper division undergraduate course which is required as a part of the common body of knowledge for all business majors. It is a four-quarter course that meets four times a week, Monday through Friday, over a period of 12 weeks. The course is organized from a behavioral/managerial viewpoint and its objectives are stated as follows:

The general goals of this course are to involve each student in:

1. a consideration of basic communications theory;
2. the study of language as a tool of management;
3. wider and more effective use of perceptions and powers of observation; and
4. developmental experiences in writing, utilizing decision-making situations as case problems.

The specific objective is to prepare each student to handle effectively the writing expected of him as a university-educated professional in the world of business.

Conceptually the goal is that the course experiences should incorporate relationships to other foundational areas of importance for students obtaining a collegiate education for business. Therefore, whenever possible, material is included which pertains to such areas as interpersonal relationships, motivation, group processes, leadership, etc.

In the effort toward this goal the decision was made in the Spring Quarter of 1972 to involve the students more intensively in the teaching/learning process through their participation in the preparation and presentation of sub-units of the course material. During the first three weeks of the term, basic information on language, semantics, composition, and communication was reviewed through lectures and discussion. Simultaneously the members of each section of BSA 305 were assigned to six groups of 5-6 students each. Members were grouped randomly; no choices on their parts were involved. This number of groups was selected because there are six basic types of situations requiring written communications which are normally covered in the course when it is taught by the lecture-discussion method. The division of the class into six groups resulted in groups of six members each in one section and five each in the other. This number of members was considered to be an effective size for an assignment involving a large amount of discussion and joint decision-making.

At the point when the students were divided into small groups, the following information was furnished to each one and a full-class question and answer session followed.

Group Number _______________ Your Name _______________

BSA 305—GROUP PROJECT

Other Members of Your Group: (Names listed)

Each group will be responsible for the class unit on one of six basic types of business letters: letter of inquiry, goodwill letter, credit letter, collection letter, unfavorable responses, and persuasive letter.

Each group is expected to accomplish the following:

1. Present to the rest of the class a consideration of the assigned type of letter.

2. Prepare a case problem to be used by the rest of the class for writing an in-class letter.

3. Evaluate the letters written by the other students.

Your presentation might consist of a lecture, a panel discussion, sharing real sample letters, having a person from the business world talk with the class, etc. Your instructor will serve as a resource person and all the materials and textbooks in her collection will be available for your use. It is planned that you use for your presentation at least one 50-minute class period but not more than two such periods. You may have materials duplicated for use in your presentation up to two pages per student enrolled in the section.

At least one class period per week will be devoted to meetings with your group. Additional meeting sessions should be arranged to the convenience of your group members. The classroom will always be available for meetings during your class time-sequence on Fridays. Each group should decide which day(s) of the week they wish to use for their presentation and for the class to write solutions.

Under this arrangement each student will write five class-completed letters and the sixth "letter" grade will depend upon the quality of your group presentation as evaluated by your peers as well as by the instructor.

Please be aware of what transpires within your group as you progress, as you will be requested to evaluate the process as we near the end of the term.

In each of the following weeks one of the six groups made its presentation, prepared the appropriate case problem, and evaluated their class-mates' solutions. The classmates then evaluated the efforts of the group in transmitting information to prepare for the class-completed case problem solutions. There was much interaction between individual students upon their sharing of these two-way evaluations.

At the end of this six weeks devoted to group presentations and written responses to case problems, the students were asked to base their individual report-writing project for the quarter on their experiences in the group project. Instructions for the report were as follows:

BSA 305—REPORT INSTRUCTIONS—SPRING

The report assignment for this term will consist of a personal summary of your group project on a certain type of letter. The format will be that presented in Chapter Nine beginning on page 244 in your text. Information on the following aspects of your group project should be included in your report:

1. A description of the project including a statement of your objective (and a presentation of the group membership).

2. A discussion of leadership in the group including the manner of selecting a leader, the reasons why you believe this particular individual was chosen, informal leadership that emerged from the group as the project progressed, the type of leadership which seemed to predominate. (You will need to read one or more journal articles or book chapters on this subject unless you are already familiar with it. A footnote should be cited at this point of your report discussion.)

3. A discussion of group processes which took place during the time you worked together—division of project into sub-assignments, conflicts which developed, positive aspects of teamwork and cooperation within the group, and overall quality of group interaction.

4. Evaluation of the project including your estimate of attainment of the group objective. Also you should include an evaluation of the learning aspects of the project for you as an individual. Did you feel that you learned more or less about letter writing from the group project as compared to receiving the presentation of another group on another type of letter? How would you compare this approach to learning to that of most of your other classes?

5. A summary statement.

Mechanics: Report should be typed if possible. Otherwise, it should be written legibly on regular weight 8.5" x 11" paper in ink (no onionskin, please). It should be double-spaced with 1" margins. The major text of the report should be five pages as a minimum. You will need to include a title page and a memorandum of transmittal.

Grading: The report will count 20 points toward your total grade and will be based on: Content (interest, coverage, organization), writing readability, appropriate and interesting choice of language, etc.), and format (including mechanics).

The evaluations of the students as reflected in their reports indicated a positive reaction to the course as taught through small group participation. Of the total of 64 students enrolled in the two sections, 50 stated that they felt the group approach had advantages over the more common lecture approach. On the other hand, only 14 indicated a negative attitude toward the concept. A few of the negatively-oriented comments were as follows:

"Group interaction can be an effective way of learning, but there is no replacement for an experienced teacher when it comes to presenting the material to the class."

"The teacher has superior knowledge and experience and is better prepared to accomplish the goals of the course."

"Not being interested in hearing other students B.S. on subjects they know little about, I found it easier to stay in my room and read the material rather than going to class. I have always liked to listen to people talk where they had a thorough knowledge of what they are talking about."

"I feel that I would prefer the classroom type of presentation by a person who had the superior knowwldge of the subject and the demonstrated ability to use this knowwldge to enhance my learning process."

"I think I could have benefitted more from this class if the work had been assigned on an individual basis. The idea of depending upon other people, partially or completely, has never been particularly appealing to me. I'm a loner and I think and react as one."

"A professional is always better than an amateur."

A sampling of the more positive comments about the group participation approach to the teaching of the course follows:

"Learning through participation versus learning through listening has many advantages. Because of the research required and the understanding necessary, the material will be retained longer by the individuals involved."

"As this course is one of the few courses in the School of Business that does not encourage direct competition between students in the class, the atmosphere is much more relaxed and renders noncompetitive attitude possible."

"By doing the digging yourself you learn whether you want to or not."

"I learned that people can work together toward a common goal with little or no difficulties if they put their minds to it."

"The barrier so often found between professor and student disappears, and a new sort of attitude prevails where students can get as much out of the course as they are willing to invest."

"This project involved interaction between students and interaction between the students and the teacher. This provided me with an opportunity to learn by sharing the work experience with my fellow students."

"One could relate on a one-to-one basis in this class. This was not a put-and-take situation, but one where feedback from teaching and students was experienced daily."

"This project made me aware that people react differently than we would like to think they do. People react individually to the written and spoken word, and having taken this class has made me even more aware of this fact."

"In this type of learning process you have to depend on others as well as yourself to gain the full benefits the class has to offer."

"There is one major benefit from the group-project approach to learning as compared to other classroom approaches: The benefit is largely learning how to perform and cooperate in a team setting."

"I was exposed, for once, to a two-way process of communication as opposed to the one-way communication that takes place in most university classrooms. It created an informal environment atmosphere which I believe is more conducive to learning."

In addition to the large number of favorable subjective comments of the students, support was also provided for the method through the results of the Student Instructional Rating System questionnaire for the Spring Quarter. In response to the statement, "You have become more competent in this area due to this course," the results were as follows:

Section 2: Strongly Agree, 32; Agree, 55; No Opinion, 5; Disagree, 9; Strongly Disagree, 0.

Section 4: Strongly Agree, 39; Agree 39; No Opinion, 11; Disagree, 6; Strongly Disagree, 0.

(These figures are expressed in terms of percentages of those enrolled in the respective sections.)

Thus, while it is recognized that improvements can definitely be made in the process of organizing a writing course in the method described in this study, the preponderance of favorable attitude would indicate that it has possibilities as a method of teaching which engages student interest and seems to provide integrative learning experiences.

C. W. Wilkinson

Grammar, Theory, and Principles in the Basic College Course in Business Communication (What? Whether? How Much?)

Teaching a basic business communication course (usually three semester hours) requires restricting its coverage for adequate depth. To avoid wasting class time on the grammar some students need, assign and mark frequent papers with coded references to needed language helps.

Limitations of class time and the slight value of results both justify spending little time on communication theory or semantics (only four points deserving attention in the basic course).

Most of the class time should go to the priciples of effective business letter psychology, tone, organization, and style. Through those principles—applied in varied kinds of letters, with follow-up on references to needed grammar helps—students will get a solid basic business communication course.

When Glenn Pearce asked me to talk on this occasion on this subject, I replied directly: "Yes, Glenn, I shall be glad to . . . ."

My reasons for responding are two: 1) I think the topic is not only highly appropriate but in need of serious consideration in ABCA; 2) I think I have something to contribute on the topic, based on long study and experience.

What I shall say, however, probably will not meet with universal agreement. In fact, I know some ABCA members will probably disagree only a little short of violently. If I'm wrong, I'm just wrong (though you can't prove it); but I ask you to realize that I'm not talking flippantly or carelessly off the top of my head. What I shall say is based on extensive study and careful consideration.

GRAMMAR

As for grammar in the basic business communications course, I first want to make clear what I interpret the rather loose term to mean. Since it involves "the study of words, their inflections, and their functions and relations in the sentence" (according to Webster's Seventh), it necessarily includes spelling, punctuation, and syntax.

With that as the general *what*, the *whether* is an easy and definite "yes." In other words, I think students need to know how to use our main tool of communication—our language—if they are to be good business communicators. And if I don't have your agreement on my positon, I certainly have the U.S. business and collegiate world's. Witness the spate of recent articles in various journals and the activities in many major universities concerned with "Why Johnny Can't Write," as *Newsweek* (December 8, 1975) titles it.

Here's a sample of them: 1) "Teaching the Boss to Write," *Business Week*, Oct. 25, 1976; 2) "Writing Crisis Spurs Big Corrective Effort," *Chronicle of Higher Education*, Oct, 18, 1976, pp. 1, 12; "The Mystery of the Business Graduate Who Can't Write," *Nation's Business*, Feb. 1977.

The last one begins thus:

> Two honor graduates of a highly regarded graduate school of business were called into a vice president's office at the company where they had been working since getting out of school a few months earlier. They were fired on the spot.
>
> Why? Neither could get down on paper in proper English as much as a two- or three-paragraph memorandum.

Bring the point home: Are you satisfied with *your* students' knowledge of grammar when they start with you?

The answers to *how much* and *how* you should teach grammar in the basic course are neither so easy nor so definite as the answer to *whether*. My answer is, "as much as the different students need." Surely you have found widely varying grammar know-how among your students in the same class. (And if you've taught in different universities, you've found different averages of grammatical competence at differenct places.) To give all those students the same instruction would be quite comparable to a doctor's prescribing the same medicine regardless of the ailment.

That practice would waste the time and money of many people. Moreover, students are as allergic to (that is, "turned off" by) unneeded instruction as patients to unsuitable medicine. The varying needs of individual students therefore prompt my answer to *how much* grammar—"as much as the different students need."

To find out who needs *what*, you could give diagnostic tests. But then where would you be? *How* would you arrange to give the proper pill(s) to each student in a varying class?

You have a better way of both diagnosing and prescribing. Surely you will require students to do lots of writing to apply the principles of business communication you're trying to teach. (Otherwise they won't learn much that will stay with them very long.) And there's your answer: In grading those papers, mark everything of importance. Don't just mark with reference to the principles that are supposedly the content of the course. Mark the writing foibles of each student with brief but specific references to sources of the specific instruction on points of grammar you want the students to learn. In other words, give some feedback.

To force the students to take the needed pills you prescribe (that is, to look up and learn the needed instruction), you will of course have to set up a penalty system with increasing severity for repetition of the same foibles. (To the extent that you can get your colleagues teaching other courses to do the same thing—even *just marking* bad writing, without the references to specific helps—you will greatly supplement and reinforce your own effects.)

You have no reason to be apologetic about any of these suggestions, either. In fact, I'd say you have more reason to apologize for abdication of duty if you don't mark bad grammar. Certainly the articles I read in business journals and the comments from business people for whom I do consulting indicate that your students' future bosses and business associates are more likely to react unfavorably to "bad grammar" than to violation of the prinicples that are the main part of our course.

For three reasons, the procedures I've explained are the most appropriate and effective ways to teach grammar in the basic business communication course:

1. The plan follows our own very important principle of adaptation. Student needs vary; therefore, we need to vary what we teach them about grammar. Only if many or most of the students in a class need the same piece of instruction would I devote class time to it.

2. The main course content—the significant principles—will make a course too full to take time out for teaching grammar.

3. Teaching grammar is most effective through illustration from a student's own writing. Trying to teach it through textbook illustration alone—or worse, as rules in the abstract—is not very effective.

Specifically, the *what* to teach (as suggested) boils down to a surprisingly few main points. The following list comes from marking an estimated 100,000 papers in basic business communication courses in eight different universities over the past forty-two years:

1. Agreement—subject/verb, pronoun/antecedent
2. Capitalization—what to capitalize and what not (specificness the general guide)
3. Comparisons—their form and logic (incomparables, incompletes)
4. Diction—particularly connotations and confusing pairs
5. Emphasis—what to stress and what to subordinate; how to do what's appropriate
6. Expletives—what they are; their generally bad effects on style; rewriting to remove most of them and make better sentences
7. Fragments—their appropriate and inappropriate uses; main cures
8. Modifiers—dangling and misplaced; English as a word-order language (the principle of proximity)
9. Punctuation—the thirteen often ignored or misunderstood pointers
10. Passives—what they are, how they hurt, how to avoid most; the active voice as the generally natural, normal, more effective way
11. Reference of pronouns—proximity, clarity, agreement
12. Sentence organization and structure (SOS)— fragments, comma splices, dangling and misplaced modifiers; simple, compound, and complex sentences in relation to emphasis and punctuation
13. Spelling (including apostrophes, which the linguistically oriented recognize as a part)—the true reasons for importance, the seven main guidelines, special attention to the 100 most frequently misspelled words in business communication
14. Unity—its meaning and methods in sentences, paragraphs, and whole pages.

Besides the frequent (and sometimes fumbling) foibles in these 14 areas, you will have occasion to mark many varied (and mostly less important) slips. The effort is little; the payoff is plentiful.

THEORY

As I did before talking about grammar, I want to make clear what *I* mean about theory. (Dr. Pearce could have well meant something more, less, or different.) To understand me clearly, however, you will need to remember that my assigned topic involves only *the basic course* in business communication and to notice the kind of course I think it should be. I think it should be a solid one in business letter writing—no more and no less. Oh, maybe a few memos for internal use, following the same principles as letters.

Certainly many existing first courses try to cover more. In fact, I know some that try to be the proverbial "all things to all men." Many try to cover general communication theory, letter writing, oral communication, and report writing, for example. They certainly are not the products of planners who know, respect, and want to offer their students a solid course. Neither a teacher nor the students can do justice to all that in the basic course. Trying to cover too much in one course leads to a mish-mash lacking the unity necessary for significant depth.

I am not saying, please notice, that oral communication and report writing are not important. I am saying, however, that anything less than a three-semester-hour course each for letters and reports leads to inadequate depth somewhere. What I am talking about here, therefore, is a sound basic course in business letters.

As for the theory in such a course, I shall distinguish between 1) business communication theory and 2) general communication theory (including explantions and models of the communication process and the whole of general semantics). So let me work backward through those points.

Yes, the course should include a little—but very little—general communication theory, and essentially no semantics. I've seen little evidence that a knowledge of semantics makes a noticeable improvement in a person's ability to write good letters.

Specifically, here are the main points that might help.

1. Our varied means of communication are all sets of symbols (such as written or spoken words and gestures, facial expressions, signals, and body movements). Communicating well depends upon a) the message sender's selecting the right symbols from the system and b) the receiver's interpreting those symbols as the sender intended. If the two don't agree closely on the meanings symbolized, we will have communication breakdown.

2. A message sender rarely if ever encodes symbols specifically representing *all* aspects of the situation. Therefore, both sender and receiver need to be alert to the Allness fallacy (Korzybski's reason for using *Etc.*). Thus, a) the sender needs to realize that unencoded aspects of context will likely influence the meaning to the receiver; and b) the receiver must (to get the whole picture) consider the whole context—the circumstances, or what we mean by "reading between the lines" and what the French mean by "the milieu."

3. Each mind is a distinctive filter which modifies its intake of symbols in special ways. Both the sender and the receiver of a message need, therefore, to realize that fact and to think in terms of "how the other person perceives the information."

4. Both senders and receivers of messages also need to be constantly alert to the possible need for adjustments because certain barriers to communication may be active (nonverbal external and internal stimuli; differences in perception, emotions, prejudices, personality, interest, and language abilities; lack of knowledge; appropriateness of the communication or the instrument of communication; competition for attention; poor organization of ideas).

Some other points of general theory (the confusions among fact, inference, and assumption; confusion of fact, prejudice, preconception, wishful thinking, projection, value judgment, and whim; and the fallacies in *is* predications, stereotying categorizations, false analogies, and polar thinking applied to continua) may be interesting speculations and good mental gymnastics. But, I repeat, I've never been able to detect any significant improvement in the communicating ability of students or teachers imbued with them. Certainly they didn't make many of our communication theorists and semanticists into good writers. Hayakawa, Chase, Johnson, Haney, and Lee, on the other hand, were good writers before they became steeped in theorizing.

To sum up, general communication theory may be worth while and may have its place somewhere; but, except for those points I've mentioned, I do not think that place is in the basic business communication course. This is because 1) it does little if any good, and 2) the limited time available should go to more practical purposes—particularly the significant business communication theory and principles.

PRINCIPLES

Since I can't cleanly separate business communication theory from the principles, I'll mix them up—maybe even use the terms interchangeably.

Yes, the basic business communication course should include some business communication theory—all those parts readily applicable to producing better letters (but not those parts specifically applicable only to oral communication or report writing.) Indeed at least 90 percent of the class time should deal with the theory and principles of business letters (including some post-mortem comments on returned papers, as more feedback.) The rest of the time should deal with some in-class writing, tests, letter form, and "course business."

(The students' out-of-class time would be for reading about these same things and writing letters to apply the learned principles and thus "make them stick." What I've already said makes obvious the use the teacher would make of a heavy out-of-class schedule—largely marking papers in terms of how well they exhibit good writing and letter principles, *with coded references to corrective instruction!*)

Those preceding statements answer, in general, all of the *what, whether,* and *how much* of principles. More specifics, however, will probably be helpful. Still in the time I have here, I must limit my specificity. With ample time I could give you 17, 97, or 197 principles, depending on how we count them. In deference to time, I'll give you broad principles, some of which subsume several attendant specifics.

Since good business letters (and hence a good basic course) are a combination of good writing, good business (*i.e.*, standard practice or justified modifications), and good attitudes and psychology, you might think we should group the principles accordingly. The classification would not be strictly logical, however, because some principles affect both *the writing* and *the psychology* almost equally.

Also the business-practice aspects hardly deserve treatment here as principles. That material is largely information, not principles; and most students will already know it or can best get it from information or directions in the cases assigned. Hence the following principles—each broad and attended by satellites, and together the main stars of the basic business communication course—are those affecting the writing and/or the psychology of letters.

My earlier discussion of grammar, of course, has to do largely with the *acceptability* of writing. Its main purpose is to bring the students' skills up to where they should have been *before* the basic business communication course. Here, on the contrary, we are more concerned with the principles of *effective* writing. And since many of these principles affect, inseparably, the psychology and the writing of good letters, they are legitimate class-time topics.

You've already heard me mention the principles of *adaptation* (in connection with handling grammar foibles) and of *controlling emphasis.* Though both are important, several others are equally or more significant.

To me the most important of all is the "you" attitude. It is often the key to successful persuasion and to achieving the proper tone and goodwill.

Planning the sequence of ideas runs a close second—deductive (direct) for readily acceptable messages; inductive (indirect, with reasons and explanations first) for disappointing or necessarily persuasive messages.

The principles of conveying courtesy, sincerity, and an attitude of service, success consciousness, and goodwill all contribute to the acceptability and effectiveness of a letter. Even keeping the writing and form of the letter inconspicuous—so that they don't distract the reader's attention from the message—is worth some attention.

For clarity, interest, and easy reading, the style of the letter should be vivid, concise, coherent, natural, and largely active voice in familiar, concrete, and specific words and short, direct sentences and paragraphs.

For effective psychology, persusion, and desirable tone, the emphasis should be on the positive (pleasant) and important points. They thus deserve emphatic beginning and/or ending positions, adequate development and independent-clause, explicit statement. Conversely, negatives (unpleasant concepts) and minor points need to be embedded (sandwiched) in middle positions, given brief treatment, and expressed in dependent clauses or phrases—or (if adequately clear) only implied.

As you see, almost every word in that brief description of the desirable letter style, tone, and psychology provides the key to one of the principles to be taught in the basic course. By the time you have taught them all, and had students write the 18 or more different kinds of letters Jack Menning once figured necessary to bring them into application (and hence firm in the students' minds), you will have given a valid course.

And in doing so you will not have class time to work on much grammar, oral communication, or report writing. With your job well done, however, your passing students will already have a long running start (and indeed be "well toward home") on what you could even dream of including about those other areas anyway.

Herman A. Estrin

Engineering Students Write Children's Books

Since Professor Herman Estrin wrote this short summary of a new teaching approach he used on his students at the New Jersey Institute of Technology he has further refined and developed his method, explained it in longer articles and presented it to writers' workshops and seminars. The approach is one that many writing teachers may want to investigate. Pointed and enforced simplicity, after all, has always been one of the central aims of the writing class.

What is surveying? How are dams built? How and where is electricity made?

Answers can be found in a series of children's books written by a group of my students at the New Jersey Institute of Technology.

In addition to improving their own writing skills, the students have taken some very complex scientific subjects and made them understandable to children.

In the engineering writing course, students must learn the importance and the means of reader adaptation. Civil engineers must write their communications to all levels—to executives and supervisors, other engineer technicians, and to the lay public.

After examining one phase of reader adaptation, introduced in the course scientific writing geared to children.

Initially, my students study content, format, and writing style of children's literature before preparing their own manuscripts.

"My first reaction to writing a children's book was a fear of the unknown," said one student. "To dabble within the mental state of a child seemed impossible. However, I learned that writing a children's science book was merely an application of what I already know about technical writing, only that I had to write this information in simple form."

"I tried to stimulate the reader by encouraging him to ask the 'why' of things," said another student. "Children seek reasons, and a world based on more reason can only be an improvement over what it is at present."

Many different questions have been posed by the student writers: "What is water pollution?" "Where is down the drain?" "Why is there electricity?" "How would you like to be an engineer?"

Other books tell about travel, solar system, highways, bridges, pollutants, and abstract concepts such as gravity and magnetic fields.

In many instances, students illustrate their own books, while others use a teamwork approach, employing the talents of friends and family members.

The books have attracted attention at the college and from children who have read them.

Natalie R. Seigle

A Game Business Communications Students Play

An invaluable multifaceted oral business communication experience that students actually enjoy. It is a simulated business seminar recorded on closed-circuit television. The general topic is selected one period in advance by the students themselves, and this helps stimulate oral communications. The sole requirement of the assignment is that each student participate in the discussion, which lasts for fifty minutes. The instructor does not take part. A student volunteer is discussion leader. The following class period, the students see and hear their own movie, and they are advised to try to judge themselves as objectively as possible. Yes, learning can be fun!

It's not a game, really. But the students think it is and it is undoubtedly one of the highlights of the oral segment of their Business Communication Course.

What is this popular game? It's a simulated business seminar and it is conducted at the audiovisual center. It is recorded on closed-circuit television and each member of the class, usually averaging 30 students, is an active participant. Each class holds and records its own seminar in one class period. The next class period they see themselves on film. This is an invaluable multilevel communications experience.

First of all, the instructor merely organizes the seminar, but takes no active part in it whatsoever. It is executed and carried through entirely by the students. Therefore, when they see "their movie" they see only themselves. The students have heard themselves speak, however, as a tape recorder has been used in class since the first week of the semester. Hearing the way their own voices sound was a first experience for most of the students and helped lay the groundwork for the simulated business seminars. With the closed television session, students had the additional opportunity to see as well as hear themselves. Each man had the chance to see himself not merely as a mirror image, but actually talking with 30 other men listening at the audiovisual session, and the same number hearing and seeing the replay at the next class meeting.

Realistically, the class cannot jointly discuss a mutual business problem for 50 minutes. They could not even discuss one for five minutes because as yet their work is purely theoretical, except for a few individuals, and their "business" problems would hardly be the same. So each class chooses its own topic, not necessarily a business subject or problem, but a topic they think they will be able to discuss intelligently for a 50-minute stint on television. We have has some startlingly good discussions on such controversial topics as Welfare, The Black Problem in Northern Colleges, Premarital Sex, The Problems of the Business Department at Providence College, National Politics, etc.

After the first bomb is dropped that *you* are going to be on TV and *you* will be expected to *talk*, there is usually a stunned silence. Then inevitably one hand will tentatively be raised and the questions asked: "You said we could talk about *any* subject?"

"Any topic at all in which you all are interested, provided that it is not indecent or immoral or slanderous." This evokes a laugh and the group begins to thaw. Suggestions of past successful discussions are thrown out to the group, and slowly ideas of their own come to them. Each group usually winds up with 12 to 24 topics, and then we proceed to narrow them. By this time enthusiasm for the project is thoroughly aroused and when the class finally votes on its subject, they all have opinions to offer. Thus, the students are moved to communicate easily and freely while the project is taking shape.

Once the topic is settled, then a group leader for the discussion is requested. It is explained to the class that the group leader of the seminar has the most difficult job but also the most rewarding. As soon as the group is "on camera," he must open this "simulated business seminar" with a brief introduction with the camera on him. But this is the easy part of the job. The difficult part lies in two areas. He must keep the discussion going and be quick to turn a loose comment into a provocative question. He must be a devil's advocate. He must also see to it that every member of the group speaks at least once. He does have some help with this, however. He has a list of the class members and if some do not volunteer or cut into the dicussion, he must call on them, checking names off as each man speaks. From the sidelines the instructor, who may know individual class members better, also can help him by sending him reminders of who has not yet spoken. An emergent leader always comes forth. And he never fails to be a good one! He takes his responsibilities seriously, often does research on the topic, and not only has a good introduction, but a fine list of leading and provocative questions to throw out if the discussion should lose some of its pace.

On the day of the seminar attendance is usually 100 percent. The men nervously file in and take seats arranged in a semicircle. The middle chair is reserved for the discussion leader. The camera is set and the operator ready. At a given signal the leader opens the discussion and ends on a questioning note. Someone always responds, and another answers. A pattern often emerges, A few, often the most unexpected ones, seem to dominate the conversation at first. It is the leader's place to see that everyone speaks, and he or she often breaks in with: "What do you think, Jim?" to a class member who has been submerged and has not spoken. The whole time the camera keeps turning on whoever speaks. After the introduction of the leader, the camera slowly moves around the group focusing for a few seconds on each face. Thus each is on camera more times than just when he is actually speaking.

By the end of the 50 minutes all class members have participated either spontaneously or by direct questioning, and the discussion is usually brought to a close most reluctantly. Usually, the class is just getting warmed up! They know it is *their* discussion, on *closed* television, and after *they* see the film the tape will be scrapped. However, all the class members are eager to return the next day to see and hear themselves on film.

The educational value of the simulated business seminar to Business Communication students is many faceted. The students enjoy intercommunication while discussing their topic. They have the learning experience of participating in a communication situation that is being recorded. They see how they sound. They are asked to mentally grade themselves on projection of personality through tonal variations, pauses, emphasis; use of facial muscles and expressions; use of hands. They are even forewarned that each student will look and wait for himself to appear on the film, that this is only natural! In addition, each student has had to communicate clearly and quickly, without planning what to say; therefore, has had an invaluable experience in "thinking and speaking on his feet."

Overall, the simulated business seminar is well worth the class time spent on it as the students increase not only their own awareness of the communication art, but also expand individual communication experience on so many levels.

Doris D. Engerrand

Teaching Oral Letter Writing

A successful method of teaching oral letter writing involves a five-step process: reading a graded letter into the microphone, reviewing the principles of good letter writing, dictating a letter from an outline, reviewing the principles of good oral practices while dictating and dictating a practice letter using these principles, and dictating a test letter. Although students listen to their dictation at each step; at step four, they put on earphones and listen not only to their letters, but also to a letter dictated with the various "don'ts" of good oral practices.

A frequent complaint of secretaries is that their bosses do not know how to dictate or that they mumble a few phrases and then tell them to "clean it up." Many executives prefer to dictate to a secretary rather than to a machine because a secretary reads back a corrected version of what they said. Many executives when confronted with the thought of facing a microphone will write the letter in longhand and then dictate it. Because of the frequency of the secretaries' complaints and because of the poor dictating habits of many executives, I decided to devote a part of my business communication class to machine dictation.

PROCEDURE

I introduce dictating after the class has spent approximately three to four weeks learning the principles of letter writing and after the students have written several letters. They are now ready to concentrate on the oral phase of the problem as I have them dictate letters covering similar problems on which they have already written letters in class.

The first assignment is to read into a microphone one of the letters they have had graded and returned to them. Students may practice at home or they may use one of the dictating units I have available for their use. This takes about one week, and it helps them get used to hearing themselves read aloud and also to dictating the punctuation.

The next step is to review the principles of good letter writing; for example, gather all relevant materials, prepare an outline, strive for conciseness, and use conversational style. After the review, the class is ready for the third step.

During this step, the students are given a letter they must answer. They prepare an outline and dictate from this outline. They are told what type of letter it will be (request, complaint), and they are allowed fifteen minutes to complete the outline and dictate the letter. During this step and during the next two steps, the students come into my office to dictate. After each student completes his or her letter, I offer suggestions on the ways to improve the dictation. Depending on class size and time devoted to office hours, this step will take from two days to one week.

The fourth step involves the principles of good oral practices while dictating. The students are given a list of do's and don'ts to study and to practice. The list includes the following:

DO

- identify yourself;
- give complete instructions including the number of carbons, type of paper, and letter style (letter, memo, report, or rough draft);
- spell all proper names and terms the secretary considers unusual;
- include all punctuation;
- dictate in phrases;
- enunciate clearly, especially word endings;
- release the button at pauses;
- proofread.

DON'T

- mumble;
- chew on a pencil or cigar or cigarette;
- walk around the room;
- breathe into the microphone;
- rock back and forth in your swivel chair.

The students are given another practice letter which they must answer. They are told in advance what type of letter it will be, and they are given fifteen minutes to complete the outline and dictate the letter. This time, however, they must include good microphone techniques. After each student dictates a letter, I again offer suggestions on ways to improve his or her technique.

At this point, I ask the student to put on earphones and to listen to a letter as a secretary does. I dictated this letter for demonstration purposes. In it I slur word endings, mumble here and there, rock back and forth in a squeaky chair, forget to release the record button, turn my head away from the microphone and add many er's and ah's. The students are amazed at what the microphone picks up. They are also more appreciative of what the secretary does. This step takes about the same length of time as step three, two days to one week.

The final step is a test. Each student is given a letter to answer, the topic of which is unknown until received. The letters are short and require relatively short answers. The student is allowed ten minutes to dictate the letter. After the dictation is completed, I listen to the letter, go over it with the student, and tell him or her the grade. I then ask the student to put on earphones and listen to the letter as the secretary would have heard it.

RESULTS

Although the students cannot be considered excellent machine dictators when they complete these series of steps, I have found that they are more relaxed when taking the test during the final step than they were during the first step. They appear to have overcome, to some extent, their mike fright. The students have indicated on their evaluations that, although they do not feel completely secure when dictating, they think that they will be able to handle routine office dictation. They feel that with a little more experience and practice, they will be able to dictate all correspondence with ease.

Doris D. Engerrand

Teaching the "You" Viewpoint

A technique proven to be successful in teaching the "you" viewpoint is a step-by-step process beginning with sentences and ending with letters. Class discussion centers around examples of student revisions shown with an opaque projector. Students rewrite five sentences for five successive days. Paragraphs to be revised are then assigned for homework for three alternating days. Letters to be revised are assigned on two alternating days followed by the answering of a letter in class using the "you" viewpoint.

We talk about writing with the "you" viewpoint, we hold class discussions about it, we give examples of "you" versus "I" writings; but do students really understand what it is? I have found that a minority of students do write and are able to write easily with the "you" viewpoint, but for others it is a real struggle. The following discussion involves a technique that I have found to be relatively successful with the student who has difficulty learning to write with the "you" viewpoint.

METHOD

After a class discussion of what the "you" viewpoint is about, I give the students five sentences at a time for five successive days to rewrite in class using the "you" viewpoint. Examples of the sentences are: "I am happy to tell you that we are sending you your new coat tomorrow," and "To help us improve our production schedules, we would appreciate your ordering two weeks in advance." The sentences are discussed and checked each day.

After completing the sentence exercises, writing with the "you" viewpoint is easier and the class is ready to try paragraphs. Prepared paragraphs are given the students to revise for homework. One paragraph is assigned each day for three alternating days. Each day following the assignment, the homework is collected, quickly scanned, and a sample chosen for viewing on the opaque projector. The students put their names on the back of the papers so no one will know whose paragraph we are viewing. The revisions are discussed during class, then later checked and returned the following day.

The class is now ready to try writing letters with the "you" viewpoint. The same technique is used at this stage as was used with the paragraphs—with one exception: prepared letters are distributed to the students on two alternating days, and they are asked to revise them for homework. A few of the letters are discussed while viewing them on the opaque projector. All the letters are checked and returned the next day. The next assignment is to answer a letter which I distribute to the students for homework using the "you" viewpoint. Again a sample is viewed on the opaque projector and discussed. All the letters are checked and returned the next day.

The final step is to have the students write a letter in class. They are given a letter to answer using the "you" viewpoint. This letter is graded and returned.

RESULTS

I have had excellent results using this technique to teach the "you" viewpoint. In fact, I have rarely had to remind a student about the "you" viewpoint in later writing after completion of these steps.

J. F. Ponthieu and James T. Watt

Broadening the Base: A New Approach to Teaching Business Communication

In an attempt to meet problems posed by rising costs and reduced staff, communications faculty at Texas Tech University developed a new method of teaching the required Managerial Communications course to approximately 400 students each semester. Each student enrolled for 2 one-hour lectures and a one-hour lab. The monster lecture sessions were team taught; and in addition, each instructor was responsible for his proportionate share of the total number of labs. This approach gave each instructor a workable number of class hours and students, and it gave each student the opportunity for individual attention and instruction in spite of the large number of students enrolled in the course.

With soaring costs and restricted budgets in education, most colleges and universities are facing the challenge of giving the best possible educational experience to students within the limited resources available. Contrary to the ideal pedagogical situations that most professors envision, meeting the budgetary constraints of a university often means large classes where the interchange between professors and students is limited. How to administer a course with 200-500 students and yet retain at least some rapport between faculty and students presents a real problem. The problem is more acute when the course is one in which the subject matter itself almost demands close proximity to students.

COURSE CONTENT AND OBJECTIVES

This was precisely the situation the staff in Managerial Communication faced at Texas Tech University when a redesign of the course from "Business Correspondence" to a wider ranging approach evolved in 1973. The content of the course was fashioned in survey manner and included: the communication process, the organizational environment and its impact on communication, the importance of knowing how to listen in business, the impact of language on communication, common erroneous assumptions leading to communication breakdowns, cultural barriers to communication, the interpretation of nonverbal behavior, and written communication. Objectives of the newly designed course included making the students aware of their communication behavior and of the principles involved; acquainting them with the ways in which communication functions within an organizational setting; and aiding them in altering patterns of communication which may be inappropriate.

The nature of the course demanded some type of interpersonal contact among students and faculty; yet with 2.5 intructors and 400 students per term, the task of creating a proximity seemed a formidable one. The fact that most students dislike the anonymity of "monster" sections and that few professors like being rather far removed from students in an auditorium situation created a real impetus for overcoming the administrative problem of designing the best learning atmosphere in restrictive circumstances.

THE "MONSTER" CLASS AND ITS SOLUTION

Teaching a large class has the advantage of disseminating basic information to a number of students at one time. It enables the maximum coverage of the subject in the shortest number of hours. Among the disadvantages that this system presents is the lack of interchange which allows students to have ample time to ask questions as in small classes and to discuss among themselves and the professor the implications of the subject at hand. Most students feel intimidated in an auditorium and are reluctant to voice questions and opinions when they occur, a situation which inhibits optimum learning. In examining the advantages and disadvantages from an administrative point of view, one would theorize that the solution would seem to lie in creating a course format which would encompass the advantages of the large class and the small class at the same time.

The format which evolved from this type of thinking was one in which both large and small classes were used. The cognitive information in the course was delivered to the students in two large auditorium classes of 200 students respectively during two lecture hours per class per week. The remaining hour of the three-hour week was devoted to smaller classes with a maximum of 30 students each. In these classes, experiential learning through cases, experiments, and practice in different methods of encoding and decoding occurred. The cognitive knowledge provided in the lectures was reinforced by experiencing its impact in the small classes and by opening an arena for discussion, questions, and interchange among the professors and students. The small classes enabled the students to come to know a professor on an individual basis and to feel that the professor knew them by more than a name or social security number on a computer printout.

This type of organization did not allow all the students to be individually exposed to each professor. It did allow each student to come to know personally at least one of the professors. Because of the limitation of a reasonable teaching load, the course was team taught with professors alternating in lecture according to the topic that each delivered. Each professor then took an equal number of small classes which allowed the students to feel that they were directly responsible to one instructor and that they had someone to call on who knew them personally when they needed outside help or had questions to be answered. This arrangement provided each professor with definite students for whom to be responsible and allowed an interface at close enough range to receive feedback from the students on the course and to amplify the areas covered in lecture.

Grading proceeded along tradional lines with 50 percent of the student's grade derived from three one-hour lecture quizzes and the remainder based on participation and performance in the small class projects. Thus, those parts of a student's grade involving subjective elements were awarded in a setting where the student was best known by the instructor.

THE TEAM TEACHING APPROACH

The professors who taught in lecture covered the small classes as well. Graduate students or assistants who did not participate as part of the lecturing team were not used. This arrangement seemed to create inner harmony and consistency within the staff itself as well as among the students in all small classes taught. The student could not feel that an outside, disinterested party conducted the small class while the policymaker in the course directed the lecture. The professor who lectured in a given area was also responsible for writing test questions for the lecture quizzes. Students did not have to wonder whose point of view would be represented on an examination. This framework allowed students to know where areas of responsibility lay.

The team teaching approach also proved advantageous for the professors. First, it provided a basis for the interchange of ideas; that is, it gave each professor a backdrop in which to place ideas before others for discussion and evaluation. Experience indicated that when one instructor presented an idea, others often could enlarge upon it, suggest alterations, or offer alternate ideas. This type of brainstorming had productive results: often the results of the group had a sum result greater than one individual alone could have provided. It also provided unity and rapport in creating and directing policy within the course. One obvious disadvantage which could occur, but did not in this situation, is a deadlock where one individual in the group feels his or her ideas are superior enough to override the opinions of others. In such a situation, team teaching would indeed prove problematical. Where instructors can work together harmoniously, special incentive and direction seem to be added to an effort to arrive at common goals.

The team teaching approach also gave the lecturers more time to develop and plan individual presentations. With each instructor giving specialized lectures, the students benefitted from more research and preparation time than they might have otherwise. The instructors came to feel that they were not competing with others on their team, but had their own area to develop and be responsible for.

PARTICIPATION THROUGH VARIETY

Responsibility in this type of course extends well beyond the province of the individual instructor. Coordination and administration of the structure and content of the course in such a way as to achieve the goals of maximum participation by each student becomes the aspiration of all instructors. Finding time within a course structure for each of 400 students to participate is a real problem, but the staff found a variety of ways in which participation could be dealt with. Most of the methods went through an evolutionary process in which they were modified to fit the existing time structure in the best possible way. The lecture periods were planned so at times there were training films which graphically illustrated communication situations within a business setting. A team of students, having already previewed the film, were then asked to serve as panelists to tie in the situations in the film to the cognitive content of the course. At times students would arrange special situations of their own to illustrate course prinicples. One team who commented on the process of polarization put "plants" from the team in the audience. They then directed a question to the audience about the possibilities of President Nixon's impeachment (in the Spring of 1974). One "plant" supported the position of impeachment; the other did not. Soon members of the audience were taking sides and polarizing the issue. As the argument reached an inflammatory level, the team members stopped the discussion and pointed out how aptly the process of polarization had been at work. A point well made!

At the end of the term, several teams of "special groups" composed situations to illustrate how communication principles function within the organization. One team had an interviewing situation and illustrated how communication can hinder or facilitate securing a job during the interview. Another team was fortunate enough to have a student member who worked at the local university television station. This team processed a set of slides with a coordinated tape which illustrated student life on the campus through verbal and nonverbal communication. These presentations were made to the large lecture classes and were quite successful. In addition, they promoted great *esprit de corps* among the groups who felt that by creating something they had received additional meaning from the course.

Variation within the course was also provided by guest speakers who came and expressed to students how communication served them in their various fields of endeavor. Local business executives, politicians, ministers, and personnel directors visited the lecture sessions and shared with students their experiences in communication. Generally, the students found persons from the "real world" of great interest and responded well to them.

In the small classes, students were provided with further diversity through business-oriented case analyses and research reports. At appointed times during the term, all students participated in group exercises to illustrate communication principles. One of the more successful exercises that students commented on was a nonverbal exercise that dealt with status determination and positive or negative feedback. (One student asked the first day of class if the course would have that exercise; he had heard about it from a student enrolled the previous semester.) The exercise consisted of pasting gummed labels on the students' foreheads, labels with various occupations from "prostitute" to "President of the United States." No student knew what the label said. Without verbal interchange, only nonverbal feedback, the students moved about giving feedback by reacting to the labels of others. At the end of the session, each student reported to the class what he or she felt that the status of his or her label was and whether feedback was positive or negative. Most were successful in interpreting the feedback accurately. Students learned something about how persons read nonverbal communication; they also found the learning a pleasurable experience.

STUDENT-FACULTY RESPONSE

For the most part, the responses of members of the faculty who have knowledge of the course have been positive. Some, who really do not seem to understand what the course is all about, feel that the time-honored positions of teaching only written business communication skills should suffice. Others are excited enough that they encourage the efforts of the staff and suggest more publication of their methods.

Business persons also tend to be receptive. Those students who have worked in business for some time appreciate the variety of knowledge that one must have about communication in order to be successful. The staff found a group of bankers to whom the course was offered very receptive to its approach.

A survey taken among 400 students in the course during the Spring term, 1974, showed that the majority of students found the course satisfactory. The highest ratings on the survey were on questions directed toward the small classes. Students still prefer them; they still like a classroom setting where they can get to know the professor and the other students.

The staff does not feel that a final resting place has been reached for their efforts. Each term brings new knowledge and ideas which modify the basic structure to some extent. Most modifications deal with giving students more time to participate. The program described has been operational for two years; doubtless, more refinements are to come. But the success of the approach taken thus far has been gratifying.

Pernell Hayes Hewing

Developing Creative Teaching Materials for Business Communication: Results of a Summer Seminar

Textbooks in business communication flood the market, but teaching materials to help the individual teacher enhance the teaching of the subject are difficult to obtain. Pernell H. Hewing has developed a Seminar to help improve the teaching of business communication. Although this seminar was developed to help improve business communication at the two-year college level, it has implications and applications for teaching business communication at all academic levels. The purposes of the Seminar were to help teachers of business communication develop creative teaching materials prepared especially for their individual classrooms and to explore common problems encountered in the teaching of business communication.

When the next Fall semester begins, some business Communication teachers will stride into their classrooms with new confidence that they will better meet the challenge of making business communication come alive in the classroom. This confidence will be bolstered by some innovative teaching materials developed in an unusual Business Communication Seminar held at the University of Wisconsin—Whitewater, in the Summer of 1973.

Business Communication teachers are aware that textbooks in business communication flood the market, but teaching materials to help the individual teacher enhance his or her teaching of the subject are difficult to obtain. Moreover, what is available may not be easily adaptable for the specific needs of the user. These two very serious shortcomings in the teaching of business communication along with the absence of books and courses on methodology and techniques of teaching business communiication have seriously impaired the teaching of this all-important course—especially at the two-year college level.

The seminar was conducted to help improve the teaching of business communication at the two-year college level; however, the seminar had implications for the teaching of business communication at all academic levels. The specific purposes of the seminar were to help teachers of business communication develop creative teaching materials prepared especially for their individual classrooms and to explore common problems encountered in the teaching of business communication.

The seminar was offered as a three-week Special Studies Course for three graduate or undergraduate credits. Some participants audited the course as they did not want credit but wanted to develop teaching materials. The seminar attracted two-year college teachers as well as high school teachers. Although the seminar was planned for business communication teachers, two of the participants were shorthand teachers who wanted to develop materials to incorporate the teaching of business communication into a shorthand course, and one participant was a data processing instructor.

A special feature of the seminar was the interaction workshop in which common problems in and special techniques of teaching business communication were shared. Participants brought along supplementary materials and handouts they use in their individual classrooms. These materials were shared while methodology and unique teaching teachniques were explored. This sharing not only provided new insight into old problems but also drew suggestions for developing teaching materials to help solve some of these problems.

The most important facet of the seminar, developing specific teaching materials for use in the participant's classroom, became a gala affair. Participants were given the opportunity to work alone or to work in teams. Each participant chose to complete an individual project for his or her specific use and to share the materials developed with other participants. Some participants developed more than one type of teaching material. The participants, therefore, left the seminar with an abundance of teaching materials as they were able to take any or all of the materials developed in the seminar. As one participant noted, "I now have a creative teaching aid for each topic I try to teach in my business communication course."

WHY A SEMINAR FOR DEVELOPING TEACHING TECHNIQUES

Although most of the materials developed were software and possibly could be found in textbooks already on the market, few textbooks adequately cover all the areas a teacher may want to cover or with the degree of attention to a specific area that an individual may desire. The business communication teacher can, therefore, develop specific material to complement the textbook. One participant in the seminar said that the textbook she uses does not contain a section on grammar and mechanics. While she favors this text over others she has reviewed, her students need help with grammar, punctuation, and the other mechanics of writing. Since this teacher could not require her students to purchase a workbook, she developed her own specially prepared material to teach grammar and mechanics.

Some of the other creative teaching materials designed in the seminar included:

1. Slides and tapes to teach employment letters and job acquisition. The 65-slide project presents a unique focus on job seeking and interviewing.
2. Learning Activity Packets to teach business letter writing in a new and exciting way. These packets could be used in conjunction with a textbook or without a textbook.
3. Special transparencies and slides on communication. This project was designed to be used to introduce communication and business communication. It has a special focus on communication theory from a practical point of view.
4. Transparencies to teach letter writing with special emphasis on teaching the beginning and endings of letters.
5. A special self-teaching manual to teach the student how to compose the business letter. This project was designed to help students who have not had a course in business communication write a letter. It can also be used to advantage with the slower student.
6. Special material to teach dictation in the classroom.
7. Tapes and transparencies to teach listening.
8. Special transparencies to teach interviewing.
9. Transparencies and script to introduce communication into a data processing class.
10. A word usage manual.

The Business Communication Seminar—Developing Creative Teaching Materials for Business Communication—was a pilot. But if the comments of the participants can be used as a barometer of success, there is a definite need to continue this effort, as this could be the answer to improving the teaching of business communication at all levels especially at the two-year college level.

The usefulness of the seminar is perhaps reflected in the words of the participant who said she enrolled in the seminar as a last chance to get some help with teaching the course in business communication which she hated. She was all prepared to go back and beg to be relieved of the burden of teaching this unwanted subject. Her comment upon leaving the seminar was, "Now I am excited about trying out some of the new ideas and new materials I received at the seminar." The data processing teacher left with the question, "Why doesn't someone develop a seminar like this one for data processing?"

Thomas M. Sawyer

Teaching Writing in a College of Engineering

Like many teachers of technical and business writing the author became one by chance and with little or no training. In a speech delivered at the Midwest Regional Conference of ABCA, Milwaukee, WI, April 22, 1977, he described his own chequered career.

His own Humanities Department serving the College of Engineering at the University of Michigan is an unusual one. There are only three other departments similar to it. He explains how it evolved.

Finally, he describes how senior engineering students in technical writing are graded by External Examiners and how they are prepared for this examination.

It is an honor and a privilege to be invited to speak to you this evening. When Professor Alred telephoned me to ask if I would speak to the American Business Communication Association meeting I was enormously flattered. I was so flattered that I neglected to point out to Professor Alred that if he had scoured the entire United States he could not have found anyone with less knowledge of business, or of the communication of business information, than myself. I am the sort of fellow who always thought an escrow was a sort of French writing table and a debenture was a kind of ice box in which one placed one's equity for fear the assets would melt and become liquid. But I had the great good fortune to marry the daughter of an Iowa banker, and shortly after we were married she caught me surreptitiously counting on my fingers as I tried valiantly to balance my checkbook. She promptly took it away from me, placed me on a niggardly allowance, and we have thrived ever since.

But Professor Alred also told me over the phone that in addition to all the prosperous business people who would be attending this conference there would be a large number of well-known, learned, and prestigious teachers of English in attendance. "You do teach writing, don't you?" he inquired. And I admitted that that is really all I have done for the past 32 years. But I couldn't bring myself to confess to him that I have taken just four college-level English courses as a student—freshman composition, a junior year course in literary criticism, a senior year course in creative writing, and a graduate survey course in drama.

I make this confession about my lack of expertise in the world of English in the hopes that you will forgive any glaring errors in my remarks and attribute them to simple ignorance on my part.

Perhaps it might be of interest to you if I told you how I happened to become, without any training, a teacher of writing, especially of scientific and technical writing. Second, I think you might be interested in a brief description of the department which employs me; after all, any outfit which employs someone like me must be peculiar, though I think they would prefer the work "unique." Third, I would like to tell you how we go about teaching both undergraduate students and practicing engineers, technical writers and editors, and practicing teachers of writing.

First, how did I become a teacher of writing? I want to discuss this because it seems to me that many, if not all, teachers of business communication, or of technical writing, got there by chance. It was sheer chance that thrust me into a career as an English teacher. In 1939 I was a senior at Kenyon College in Gambier, Ohio, a lovely little village five miles from anywhere, and a tiny, Oxford-like college of 300 all male students. I was a Biology major, and a good one. Even today if you hand me the embalmed carcass of a cat, I can show you the greater trochanter of the humerus in a trice. I had a stable, in small bottles of course, of red-eyed and white-eyed fruitflies which I bred assiduously.

Since there were no female students at Kenyon College and no females in the village of Gambier except the wives of Kenyon faculty or the daughter of the local greengrocer, after a long day of slicing frog livers into tissue-thin slices for microscope slides I expended my excess youthful energies in Thespian activities, largely because the local ladies were the only source of actresses and many of the play scripts called upon one of the student actors to clasp, even to kiss, one of these ladies. I distinctly recall my Political Science professor announcing to the class, while leering at me, "If some people don't keep their hands off my wife, they're going to flunk this course!"

It was this excess energy which led me to take a course in creative writing with John Crowe Ransom. I knew nothing at all about him except that he seemed to enjoy considerable status as the editor of the *Kenyon Review* and some of the newspapers and news magazines seemed to have heard of him.

There were only about six of us in this creative writing class—me and five nonbiologists, such as: Robie Macauley, now fiction editor of *Playboy* magazine; Peter Taylor, whose short stories were later to appear in *New Yorker;* and the late Robert Lowell, who later made a name for himself as a poet. In Ransom's seminar I too wrote poetry—for the simple, practical reason that it took less time and paper to produce two or three lyrics than it did to devise a 20- or 30-page short story.

But alas! I graduated from this idyllic ivory tower in June 1939 and headed into the world of business, which in those days seemed strangely unreceptive to lyric poets, amateur actors, or even frog liver slicers. I ended up in Toledo, Ohio, working 12 hours a day for fifty cents an hour as a machinist turning out copper commutators for electric motors in a factory which would probably remind many of you of a scene from one of Charles Dickens's novels. I'm afraid that that experience has contaminated my attitude towards Toledo, Ohio, ever since.

After a full year of this seamy sort of life, I received a letter from the Alumni Secretary of Kenyon College telling me that a preparatory school in Honolulu, Hawaii, was looking for a Biology teacher. Would I care to apply?

Would I care to apply! With visions of palm trees, white sands, and dusky hula girls, I dashed off a letter of application immediately. Clearly I needed some letters of recommendation. My Biology professor was an obvious choice. The President of Kenyon College was another. You must remember that the college was small enough that every student knew the President.

But two letters, like a two-legged stool, felt unbalanced. I needed a third. So I asked our academic star, John Crowe Ransom, for a letter as well.

Months passed in Dickensian gloom, then one day I received a cablegram—my very first *cablegram!* (Come to think of it, the only cablegram I have ever received.) It said: "Offer you a job teaching English. Nine hundred dollars a year."

I was flabbergasted! I was a Biologist. Well, yes I was temporarily a machinist, but I thought of myself as a Biologist. What were they doing offering me a job teaching English? I didn't know anything about that.

But anything was better than making commutators in Toledo, Ohio. I promptly cabled back: "I accept. But why English?"

It turned out that Headmaster Stone of Iolani School in Honolulu had already hired a Biology teacher by the time my application arrived. But in the meantime a hot-blooded young English teacher had made a pass at the Headmaster's blonde and nubile daughter and had been abruptly and untimely dismissed. With the start of the school year rapidly approaching, the Headmaster had riffled through the applications on his desk looking for a replacement, had stumbled across Professor Ransom's generous letter of recommendation in my behalf, and decided to take a chance on me.

You may well remark upon the paucity of my training for such a position—especially in light of the fact that the students I was about to face—all boys—were evenly distributed among those from Japanese, Chinese, Portuguese, Korean, Hawaiian, and Haole (the Hawaiian word for "stranger" or white man) family backgrounds. Indeed I taught every last thing I knew in the first fifteen minutes of the first class, I had nothing left to say—not for the rest of the hour, not for the rest of the day, not for the rest of the week, not for the rest of the year.

But Headmaster Stone had been a missionary in China and he was, when I knew him, a Major in the Chaplain Corps of the U.S. Army. He knew something about the teaching of the English language to boys whose native language was not English. And he knew something about training untrained teachers like myself to teach such boys. He required me to turn in to him each week a detailed outline of what I planned to do the coming week in each of my five classes of 25 boys. And each week I was expected to assign, receive, read, mark-up in detail, and grade a composition from each and every student. Thus he expected me to grade 125 compositions every week. And he asked me to submit sample batches of compositions to him at frequent intervals so that he could check up on how well I was reading and marking up all those papers.

As you will appreciate, I saw a great deal less of those palm trees, white sands, and dusky hula girls than I had anticipated. This was the only instruction I have ever received in how to teach writing. Headmaster Stone taught me an invaluable lesson. I had, and have, never worked so hard in my life. But after 32 years I still believe that it is essential to plan out, and on paper for all to see, what you hope to accomplish in every class meeting. And I still believe that it is essential that the students write a composition every single week. My senior Engineering students write a paper or deliver a speech every single week during the term, but, fortunately, I have fewer than the 125 I had in Honolulu.

Pearl Harbor Day closed all the schools in Hawaii so I became in rapid succession: a Red Cross First Aid Instructor; and teacher of Speech and Drama back at Kenyon College again (perhaps because I had kissed so many faculty wives); an ambulance driver with the American Field Service attached to the British 14th Army in Burma, the 8th Army in Italy, and the 21st Army Group in Belgium and Holland. In 1945 I was back in Ann Arbor, Michigan, once more a machinist as I had been in Toledo, hoping, despite the lack of G.I. Bill benefits, to work my way through graduate school while working on the night shift as a punch-press operator for a ball bearing company in Ann Arbor. And once again I became a teacher entirely by chance.

As I was preparing to register as a graduate student in Speech, I was suddenly tapped on the shoulder by the Chairman of the English Department of the College of Engineering who asked if I would like to teach freshman speech and freshman composition to engineering students. Although I had been a punch-press operator for only a week and a half, I had already decided that I preferred pushing a pencil to pushing a greasy strip of steel plate. So I again said yes.

The English Department of the College of Engineering changed its name to Humanities Department in 1968, but it still remains a peculiar and unique institution. On the Ann Arbor campus of the University of Michigan, with 33,000 students, 17 different schools and colleges, and 155 different graduate degree programs, the Humanities Department with a professorial staff of 24 is the one and only purely service department—that is, a department which has no students of its own. The University also has a large, graduate English Department with a professorial staff of about 70 which serves the rest of the campus. Only three other universities that I know of have similar arrangements. The Engineering Colleges of the Universities of Washington and Virginia and the College of Agriculture of the University of Minnesota maintain separate departments to teach their students literature and composition.

Why should the College of Engineering at Michigan have a separate department? Like my own teaching career it is partly due to chance. Originally the university had a single English Department to serve all students. But in 1889 Professor Fred Newton Scott was brought to Ann Arbor and he combined great vigor with a great interest in teaching writing. In 1903 he helped to establish a Department of Rhetoric, concentrating on teaching writing rather than literature. Professor Scott also brought to Ann Arbor an expert in engineering report writing, Professor J. Raleigh Nelson, who became the first chairman of what was popularly known as "Engineering English" in 1908. Unfortunately, Professor Scott retired in 1930 and the Department of Rhetoric was merged with the Department of English. From the point of view of the College of Engineering that date may perhaps mark the beginning of the subsidence in the level of the writing ability of students—nonengineering students, that is.

But as a matter of fact when I joined the Engineering English Department in 1945 it was difficult to detect any differences between it and the larger, more prestigious English Department across the campus, except that it was smaller and offered fewer courses. Although the College didn't object if the Department offered some undergraduate survey courses in literature, it considered our principal function to be teaching students how to write. Since the engineering faculty didn't know much about teaching writing, they left it up to us. However, most of our faculty didn't know much about teaching writing either. Most of the professorial staff were graduates of English departments and consequently had taken about as many courses in teaching writing as I had—none. J. Raleigh Nelson had retired; only one professor was left who taught report writing and he was near retirement and not very popular with the students anyway. The staff consisted of 7 Professors, 4 Instructors finishing their Ph.D.'s in literature, and 17 graduate student Teaching Fellows like myself because the College had a booming enrollment of returning G.I. veterans.

So we taught writing the way everyone else did, and most English departments still do—we taught freshman composition. First year engineers took two terms of composition and one term of speech for six hours of credit. Upperclassman took two more two-hour courses in literature—a total package of 10 credit hours.

If the department had continued on this course I believe that the prospects for our continued existence as a separate department would now be dismal indeed. We were doing nothing that could not have been done just as well by the English Department across the campus. Of course we argued that we did it better because we had a special affinity for undergraduate students, but today as graduate enrollments in English plummet, the department across the campus is rapidly developing the same affinity—although it seems to be a painful process.

Fortunately we did not continue on the same course and today we can argue that we really do provide a unique and special service. Several factors led us to change our program.

First, when our one report writing teacher retired some of his younger colleagues were drafted to take over this senior-level elective course. They had no preconceptions about how it should be taught because they had no training in such teaching, so they approached it fresh, consulted with the engineering faculty about what should be required, discovered to their surprise that these engineers simply wanted engineering reports written in such a way that any educated person could read and understand them, and found that as educated laymen themselves, the course was interesting to teach. W. Earl Britton was one of these younger men, and some of you may have read, among his other articles, his argument "The Trouble With Technical Writing is Freshman Composition" in the book, *The Teaching of Technical Writing* published by the National Council of Teachers of English. As Britton learned, senior engineering students, unlike freshmen, had a great deal of interesting information, and, again unlike freshmen, they were trying to convey it to an educated layman—their English teacher. Freshmen are always writing to people who know more than they do. Britton became so interested in this communication problem that he organized a summer conference course for engineers for industry, and the course is now in its 20th year and has on occasion enrolled as many as 90 participants.

Second, in 1957 Sputnik went into orbit and shortly thereafter so did engineering research in the United States. One of the major centers for research in radar and infrared scanning devices was Willow Run Laboratories at the University of Michigan. They began to produce a flood of reports of experiments and of new technical developments and needed a number of technical editors to help with these manuscripts. So some of us were offered part-time editorial work in these laboratories. We found that it was fun trying to help such people as Emmett

Leith, who developed the new technique of holography, explain what it was he was doing. Thus several more of us became interested in scientific and technical writing.

But the most important factor was the establishment in 1965 of a special committee in the College of Engineering charged with shortening the entire curriculum to enable a student to graduate in four years, rather than four and a half or five. Every department, including Engineering English, was represented on this committee and we were given *carte blanche.* "Forget about tradition," we were told, "propose the sorts and arrangements of courses you think would be ideal." A golden opportunity!

So we thought hard about it. We all disliked freshman composition, and so did the students. It was drudgery for both student and teacher. We all thought that six hours of Great Books—the *Iliad*, *Oedipus*, the Platonic Dialogues, Dante, Chaucer, Shakespeare, *The Federalist Papers*, and the like—would be better for freshmen who know so little of our cultural heritage and who are too young to have acquired sufficient information or experience to have anything to write about that is worth reading. Moreover, Great Books would be much more fun to teach.

Rather naturally each English teacher had his own literary specialty that he wanted to teach, so a required course in literature for upperclassman was proposed.

But what were we going to do about writing and speaking? The engineering faculty would certainly never agree to a program devoted entirely to literature and without training in communication.

Then a very simple and sensible idea occurred to us. Why not require all *seniors* to take a course in writing and speaking? Those of us who had acquired some experience in teaching technical writing and in doing scientific editing honestly enjoyed such work. Why not simply turn our traditional arrangement of courses upside down? Great Books for freshman, composition for seniors, and literature in between. No one else we knew of had an arrangement like this, but why not take a chance?

This is what we proposed to the College and they accepted it. When the new curriculum was adopted in 1967 we became the only department in the entire College to be allocated more hours, rather than fewer—12 hours as opposed to our original ten. And once the new curriculum was approved, we argued that our new program was so superior to our old one that we deserved a new name to signalize this reincarnation. The University Regents agreed and in 1968 rechristened us the Humanities Department of the College of Engineering.

Frankly I think our program is one that every English department should adopt. Courses in communication should be offered when the student needs them, and that is when he is a senior and has acquired a body of knowledge about his chosen specialty and is about to go forth and try to apply it. He will need to communicate to others what he knows, and he will need to persuade them to use the esoteric skills he now possesses. If he cannot communicate that knowledge, if he cannot persuade people that his skills are applicable, he will indeed be helpless.

How do we try to meet this student's needs? Since I just finished the final examination in my own Scientific and Technical Communication course last Wednesday night, perhaps a description of this examiniation may be illuminating.

This term I had 33 seniors: Mechanical Engineers, Chemical Engineers, Civil Engineers, Nuclear Engineers, Metallurgical Engineers, Electrical Engineers, Computer Engineers, and Naval Architects. We often enroll students from other colleges as well, such as Nursing, Pharmacy, Public Health. This term I had a Zoologist and a major in Natural Resources. The list of topics they were writing and talking about is too long to recite here, but here are some examples:

'Powder Diffraction: Debyr-Scherrer Technique for Compound Identification," "Electromagnetic Pulse Effects on Aircraft: Analysis of Surface Fields on Models," "Icebreaker Hull for the Great Lakes: A Preliminary Design," "Essential Hypertension: Renin-Sodium Profiling as a Basis for Treatment," "Pulsed TEA CO_2 Lasers: Design and Principles of Construction."

The examination these students faced was really a very simple one. Each student submitted two copies of his final written report, one to be read by an engineer from an industry in Ann Arbor—such as Mr. William Amey, Control Systems Specialist for the Bechtel Power Corporation—the other to be read by a technical writer or editor from an industry in Ann Arbor—such as Mr. James McGraw, Technical Editor for Manufacturing Data Systems. Each of these examiners also came in the evening to listen to the students give a 10-minute public lecture on the same topic. There they, and the other members of the audience, could ask the students any questions they wished. These public lectures were also videotaped and in a week or so, after the students had an opportunity to see their lectures themselves, they were broadcast over Ann Arbor's Cable TV system for the whole city to see and hear.

It is the two examiners—Mr. Amey and Mr. McGraw, for example—who will decide what the students' final grades should be. Since they are still studying the students' written reports, I don't yet know how my students made out, but I can assure you that I am in the same nervous sweat the students are.

As you can probably guess, the whole of the term is spent in practice for this final test. The students write parts and pieces of their final reports and distribute them to the other students for critical comments. It becomes pretty obvious that if the Zoologist and the Civil Engineer can't understand pulsed TEA CO_2 lasers, the Nuclear Engineer better work hard on his explanation so that it will be clear to Mr. Amey and Mr. McGraw. My function is to help, and for this reason I think it's only fair that Mr. Amey and Mr. McGraw evaluate me too and submit a grade for me to my Departmental Chairman and my Dean. Last December, for 41 students, the examiners awarded an overall average grade of 3.2, or just better than a *B* for the whole group. Eight students got *A's* from both examiners, and 14 got an *A* from one and a *B* from the other. The Dean hasn't yet told me what grade I got.

I am sure that you are all aware of C. P. Snow's argument that there are now two distinct cultures—the culture of science and technology and the culture of literature and the humanities. I am doing my best to help scientists and engineers make themselves comprehensible to people on the other side.

But since I am speaking to the American Business Communication Association it occurs to me that there may be a third culture—the culture of business. And business is relying more and more on the computers that my engineers produce. You can program a computer to do a lot of interesting things, even to write a manuscript for you. Here is a sample of what Lexar Company of Los Angeles can get the computer to write if it programs it to choose a random batch of words and link them together following grammatical rules. See if this doesn't almost sound as if it meant something:

> Parallel organizational capability may always be compared with a continuous search for optimal interaction; often the product configuration encompasses any phased requirements. A specific

example magnifies the importance of inherent infrastructure contraints.

But here is a sample of business writing which may, only may, have been written by a human being. It is a notice my wife received from a local department store, and I read it in full:

> Any holder of this consumer credit contract is subject to all claims and defenses which the debtor could assert against the seller of goods or services obtained pursuant hereto or with the proceeds hereof. Recovery hereunder by the debtor shall not exceed amounts paid by the debtor hereunder.

I am sure that you all know what that means, and I would very much appreciate it if you would assist the author thereof in making himself comprehensible to us less fortunate creatures who come from an alien culture.

Jo Ann Hennington

Role Playing: An Excellent Option for Teaching Job Interviewing Techniques

Alert business communication professors are continually seeking for new ways to teach interviewing techniques to students who will soon be competing for positions in the job market. The development and use of role playing situations in business communication classes can be a powerful and motivational teaching method for teaching job interviewing. Try this creative teaching technique to help students develop interviewing strategies for job seeking.

"Interviews are an important part of being employed—there needs to be a unit on preparing students how to interview." "Teachers needs to teach students how to interview because students seem to be uneasy when interviewing." "Students need to learn how to communicate during an interview." "Students are better prepared for the actual job interview when they have participated in role playing situations."

Professors often hear comments similar to these from personnel directors with whom they have discussed job interviewing. The above unedited comments from business executives indicate that students entering the job market today need to be equipped with good interviewing techniques in order to become successful in the job interview.

One successful option currently being used in teaching collegiate business communication students interviewing techniques is the use of role playing.

ADVANTAGES OF ROLE PLAYING

Learning by doing is the basis of many classroom activities. The involvement of students in role playing interviews places them in another person's position so that they may better see how other people view the interview situation. Role playing can become an effective part of an interviewing unit. The advantages of role playing interviews are appealing to business students because:

1. It allows every member of the class opportunity for active participation in the interview situation.
2. It helps to develop positive interviewing techniques.
3. It helps the students in their understanding of other people's feelings and attitudes in the interview.
4. It helps students to understand themselves as they interview for job openings.
5. It allows students to experience interview situations they will face when actually job seeking.
6. It develops interviewing and questioning skills needed in spontaneous verbal interaction.
7. It provides concrete examples of behavior as a basis for further class discussion on interviewing techniques.

Furthermore, role playing will appeal to students in the classroom because they are natural actors. Professors are able to use students' natural acting ability as an effective tool to help students learn effective interviewing techniques.

WHERE TO BEGIN

To prepare for the role playing interviews, have the students listen to lectures and tapes about job interviewing and effective interviewing techniques; complete background reading in the library from a reading list on job interviewing; check out cassettes and listen to model interview situations; look at training films depicting job interviews; and read pamphlets, materials, and brochures published by business firms dealing with their respective job requirements.

TEACHING WITH THE ROLE PLAYING SITUATION

Divide the students in small groups of 3 or 4 individuals. Give each group a certain interview situation and ask them to act out how they think each person in that situation will respond by putting themselves into that person's place. Through their acting, students will try to speak and feel as they think those persons in the interview situation would. By doing, the students learn to see the situation from other persons' viewpoints, thereby enabling the students to better understand others in the interview situation.

The members in each group then prepare for role playing their interview session by writing the dialogue between the interviewer, the interviewee, or any other characters needed for the role playing situation. The students need to meet several times outside the regular class time to plan and practice their role playing situations.

All role playing situations are designed as small group activities rather than individual exercises, and the participants will need to discuss their cases at length as a group. Having the students discuss and prepare the cases within their peer group usually produces more involvement and critical thinking.

After the students prepare their role playing situations, one or two class periods are used for the groups to present their situations to the entire class. As each group acts out their situation, the professor can then involve the other groups by asking if anyone knows of another way the situation may have been done (note—*another* way—not a *better* way). The professor should be careful not to give an interpretation of the one correct way an interview should be done. The way the situations develop and end should depend solely on the students' own view of the roles they are playing. The professor is simply the director of learning and decides when the activities of a group are finished, the alternatives are decided, or when the dialogue terminates.

HOW TO END

Each role playing situation ends with a discussion and comment sessions where the students are encouraged to relate similar experiences they have had when interviewing or to describe positions they have been offered as a result of employment interviews.

Also at the end of each role playing session, each role playing group is evaluated by the other students, using an interview evaluation form such as the one below. The interview evaluation sheet for each group is then discussed by the entire class. This is the opportunity for each of the groups to get feedback information on their interviewing incidents. The class should cover each incident, gleaning good interviewing techniques from each case.

After each group has taken its turn with the interviewing situation, the students are able to see, feel, and even express what it was like to be interviewed or to do the interviewing. Many good interviewing techniques can be reinforced with these role playing situations. These role playing situations present and create problems that the students will probably face during actual interview situations.

CONCLUSION

The alert communication professor is always interested in new options for teaching job interviewing. Role playing can be a powerful and motivational teaching method. Potentially, role playing is a dynamic and effective teaching method whereby each member of the communications class is actively participating. Role playing can be a very interesting and creative teaching method; its uses in interviewing situations are limited only by the creativity of the individual professor.

BUSINESS COMMUNICATIONS INTERVIEW EVALUATION SHEET

YOUR NAME:____________________________________

INTERVIEW GROUP:______________________________

Please fill out one form for each interview group.

1. Which of the following describes the role of the interviewer?
   _________ Tell and sell.
   _________ Listen and agree.
   _________ Listen, no input.
   _________ Mutual input (balanced).
2. Which of the following describes the role of the interviewee?
   _________ Tell and sell.
   _________ Listen and agree.

_________ Listen, no input.
_________ Mutual input (balanced).

3. How well did the interviewee maintain eye contact with the interviewer?
_________ Good eye contact.
_________ Wandered.
_________ Darted.
_________ Stared.
4. How well did the interviewee listen to the interviewer?
_________ Very well.
_________ Well.
_________ Poorly.
_________ Very poorly.
5. Which of the following describes the appearance of the interviewee?
_________ Strong, positive appearance.
_________ Less, positive appearance.
_________ Neutral appearance.
_________ Negative appearance.
6. The Interview atmosphere was:
Unpleasant ________________________ Pleasant
Rushed ________________________ Relaxed
Confusing ________________________ Clear
Hostile ________________________ Friendly
Structured ________________________ Unstructured
Blunt ________________________ Tactful
Suspicious ________________________ Trustful
Nervous ________________________ Composed
Uncooperative ________________________ Cooperative
Quiet ________________________ Enthusiastic
7. List any other comments about the interview. ____________
____
____

Juanita Williams Dudley

A New String for an Old Bow: Business Writing with Journalistic Applications

For over 22 years, Purdue's Department of English has offered a course for students who hope to obtain jobs in which either a major or collateral duty is disseminating information to nontechnical audiences, often about technical subjects, via company or industry publications. Students are asked to: make group analyses of house journals and annual reports, write articles for prescribed audiences, produce a class newsletter simulating a house journal, prepare a letter of application for a specific job, produce an information sheet, and write a paper analyzing either the style of a business publication or the state of the job market in the student's particular field.

From 1944 to 1946, Professor Vic Gibbons of Purdue's Department of English took a leave of absence to work as an editor of a trade magazine entitled *Plastics* published by Ziff-Davis Publishing Company, and as a technical writer for Owens-Corning Fibreglass, where his job was to make requests for an expanded research budget so straightforward and persuasive that they appealed equally to the board of directors and the engineering staff. As a consequence of this stint in the workaday world, the professor conceived a new course—English 515 (Business Writing: Journalistic Applications)—and, upon his return to Purdue, implemented it.

The course, which is designed to inculcate the principles of good house and trade journalism as well as sundry other writing and editing skills, rapidly developed a steady and enthusiastic clientele among students majoring in public relations, agricultural journalism, industrial journalism, industrial administration, home economics, engineering, and pharmacy. It is an exciting permutation of basic communication skills learned in freshman English and a course devoted primarily to letter and report writing. Almost all the students enrolled expect to obtain jobs in which either a major or collateral duty is disseminating information to nontechnical audiences, often about technical subjects, via company or industry publications, news releases, abstracts, annual reports, and policy statements.

After Professor Gibbons retired, Glenn E. Griffin, former president of ABCA, took over the course, and when Professor Griffin retired, I was fortunate enough to inherit it. Because I believe that the skills taught in the course are highly marketable and that most teachers of business writing have the competence, usually as the result of consulting work, to teach these skills, I would like to describe the content of the course and the techniques that have served me well in teaching English 515.

BACKGROUND READING

Students are told at the outset that they must regularly read one business publication weekly—for example, the financial section of the *New York Times*, the *Wall Street Journal*, or *Business Week*—and they are assigned, in groups, analyses of a particular house journal or a complex of company publications. They are asked to assess the assigned publications for general level of reading difficulty (running a Gunning Fog Index on several copies), style, ostensible audience, length and kind of features, the nature of appropriate filler, makeup, and editorial policy. Where copies of a variety of publications within a complex are available, each student is given several copies of—let us say—a regional newsletter, a national employees' magazine, and an international newspaper. The group then, after presenting an analysis of various publications, makes inferences about journal requirements for a variety of audiences—for example, consumers of a particular product or employees—both active and retired—and their families.

Editorial policy becomes an engrossing study for the class as they listen to reports on journals which reflect a highly paternalistic attitude on the part of management or—as is the case of the exemplary *Bankamerican*—embody the belief that a good house journal aims at informing employees about what their co-workers are doing and new developments within the company itself.

A scrutiny of the stories featured in the journals soon makes the students aware that virutally anything is a suitable topic for an employees' magazine—from a recipe for macaroni salad to a canvass of working couples on the subject of division of labor within the home. And through the analyses of employee journals, the relevance of retiree-oriented features, as well as non-technical descriptions of recent developments in company products and services, becomes obvious.

Precisely *because* the house journal is as eclectic as it is, the first assigned feature may be based on a particular interest, knowledge, or expertise of the student. In private conferences, the students and I brainstorm their experience for likely feature topics. Then, with the *Writer's Market*, as well as a roster of house and trade journals, at hand, we locate what seems an appropriate target market for the planned story. In perusing *Writer's Market*, the student once again has his or her attention directed to intended audience, length of acceptable stories, preferred style, and editorial policy. (I find that a student writing for a specific market has far less difficulty in conceiving and developing an article than one writing in a vacuum.)

In the course of the conference I give a prescriptive recipe for a feature story—lead, slant, body, and conclusions.

I make no apologies for the prescription, explaining that, once the writer has become a professional rather than an amateur, he or she may venture to experiment with organization and structure but that, while still a tyro at writing feature stories, it is best to be guided by a serviceable formula.

STARTING TO WRITE

For many students English 515 is the first composition course taken since freshman English. Hence, first drafts of their first feature stories are apt to be tedious in that they are comprised of lacklustre generalizations and tantalizing references to specific instances without adequate illustration or example. Many also abound in overlong paragraphs made up of primer-style sentences. A few are mechanically inept. Virtually none contain dialogue or description to bring a scene or circumstance to life.

And in a dismaying number of cases, the bodies of the stories bear no visible resemblance to the slant, or implied purpose, of the article.

Accordingly, I duplicate copies of half a dozen stories (always presented in class anonymously) and assign their reading for homework. Along with the stories I distribute a sheet listing standards for evaluation of the piece—namely, general interest, overall organization (including logical development of the central idea and coherence and continuity), paragraph and sentence structure, mechanics, and style. Of all deficiencies, a lack of interest calls itself first to a reader's attention, and complaints about dullness furnish me, early on, with a splendid excuse for introducing instruction in narrative technique and writing dialogue and description. Glaring errors in sentence structure, grammar, and mechanics evoke polite condemnation from the more literate members of the class, thus alerting the offending authors to the need for a good handbook. And a plethora of commas supplies me with a chance to call attention to the fact that while many high school and freshman English teachers proscribed the dash, it is a good and useful—indeed, often a sophisticated—mark of punctuation, as are the colon, the semi-colon, and parentheses.

The second drafts of these first stories display imagination and a beginning virtuosity. For example, the lead in a story about a 4-H sewing class opened, in the first version, with these uninspired sentences:

> Summers are meant for spending long relaxing days outdoors with friends. Swimming, biking, playing ball, and visiting friends are just a few of the many ways girls enjoy summer days. Who would ever think learning to sew could be as much fun as these other activities? Perry Township 4-H club members think so!

After the lecture on narrative techniques, the author revised her introduction to read:

> My wooden-soled sandals clicked against the terrazzo floor and the sound echoed back from the long rows of empty lockers lining the hall as I walked to the classroom. A blast of heated air greeted me when I turned the key in the lock and pushed open the door to enter the silent room. It was only eight-thirty in the morning, but already the temperature was ninety-three degrees. I pulled the draperies closed against the blaring sun, switched on the fluorescent lights and began to ready the room for the day's activity.
>
> While I opened the supply cabinets, brought chairs down from their table-top perches, and set up the pressing equipment, I wondered

> if anyone would come. Surely the weather was just too unbearable to consider doing anything other than relaxing. Much to my surprise, however, 4-H members considered learning to sew a good way to spend that particular day, as well as many that followed. Twenty-three girls showed up!

The second assignment, a personal profile, supplies an excuse to bring in a working newspaperman or woman, who lectures to the class on interviewing techniques. Professional newspeople are more than generous with their time and happily explain ways in which to get taciturn subjects to open up and elaborate on their experiences, as well as the necessity for quoting accurately and being selective in the choice of material to incorporate in the finished story. One guest speaker was particularly helpful in explaining how careful description of the background against which a subject was interviewed could make a contribution to the story's total effect—for instance, grimey filling-station paraphernalia contrasted with the "tapering, translucent hands" of the fairy-princess-like blonde who owned and operated the station.

Following the lecture by the newperson, I invite a real subject to class for a "press conference"—in most instances, a retiree. (University communities abound in lively, interesting retirees.) And group critiques of finished stories call attention to the importance of specific descriptive detail, the necessity for judicious, accurate quotation, and the way that a combination of detail, quotation, and editorial comment convey the essence of a subject.

After the profile assignment, I ask the class to produce, again in groups, a newsletter for the class, by name *The Five-Fifteener*. To give students a professional perspective, I invite a director of public relations from a local bank—a man whose entry into the world of public relations was the result of his stewardhip for in-house publications and "dog and pony shows" designed to inform the public about the variety of services offered by Lafayette National. Or I cajole into speaking to the class members of the staff of *Perspective*, a Purdue newsletter sent to all alumni, parents of students, faculty and staff, and "friends of the University."

I ask the students to equate English 515 with a company, their classmates with employees, and me with management. The objectives of *The Five-Fifteener* are specified as those of any good in-house journal: to inform the reader of the company's recent, present, and future activites; to enhance rapport among employees; and to effect and maintain good rapport between employees and management. The finished products—usually four separate issues of the newsletter—are duplicated and distributed to all members of the class, and the various groups then critique the papers according to the avowed objectives in the masthead, as well as criteria formulated in general class discussion. A happy by-product of this assignment is a sense of camaraderie within the class that transcends the usual classroom relationship.

Following the newsletter assignment, I ask students to write letters of application for jobs. They have been members of the class long enough by this juncture to feel that they have developed some new marketable skills, and crow with delight as they locate openings in which editorial talents would be an asset.

To give the class a pragmatic view of finding a job, I invite as a speaker the assistant to the director of Purdue's placement office, who apprises the class of the latest feedback from employees on information preferred in letters and data sheets. I also duplicate and distribute some of the excellent advice featured in *The ABCA Bulletin*—especially the Mansfield article on resumes in *The ABCA Bulletin*, September 1976. And, as in the instructions on writing an article, I stress the importance of a slant—a focusing on those attributes and talents that accord with the objectives and needs of the company to which the application is applying—in other words, adapting the "what I can do for *you*" approach to the applicant's abilities and ambitions.

The analysis of the annual report is the next assignment. Students are given a number of reports from a variety of industries to examine for effective presentation of: 1) highlights, 2) statement of policy from the president or chairman of the board, 3) overview of the year's operations, 4) financial statement and notes, and 5) a cursory description of management personnel. This assignment not only focuses attention on the necessity for a readable format; it also emphasizes the importance of lively, lucid prose in explaining a company's achievements and goals. It is, moreover, an occasion for lecture on and demonstration of proper techniques of presenting, via graphic aids, a variety of quantitative data.

Toward the end of the semester, when schedules are crowded and interview trips take precedence over class-room activities, I assign the abstracting exercise and information sheet. Neither of these assignments requires the legwork and sustained effort that the first feature stories do, and, although mastery of abstracting skills is no small feat, students seem, at this time, to welcome an exercise requiring mere reduction rather than conceptualization.

The benefits of abstracting are so immediately perceptible, however, that I confess to having toyed with the idea of beginning the course with the exercise. No other project seems as effective in teaching people to prune their prose and firm up their style. The necessity for reducing a body of prose to from five to ten percent of the total number of words in the original sample implies that the instructor must inevitably discuss topic sentences, methods of development within the paragraph, and devices for transition and continuity. Although these subjects have been discussed at length in connection with the feature stories, they are now seen as being particularly relevant to the duties of a business communicator, who may, in the early stages of his or her career, have to reduce lengthy documents to capsule summaries for busy supervisors and executives.

With the aid of a pamphlet produced by Phoenix Mutual Life, entitled *Your Business and Your Taxes*, I have challenged classes to do painstaking reading and scrupulous abstracting. The content of the pamphlet, incidentally, fascinates public relations majors, many of whom lack familiarity with corporate structure but hope one day to become pivotal parts of same. In general, teaching abstracting is not an easy task, but with the aid of transparencies and an overhead projector, comparison between the original passage and various reductions is made easy, and a demonstration of the way I proceed to abstract a piece of prose serves to eliminate a good deal of student trepidation over the assignment.

The final assignment is either an article on the state of the job market in the student's particular field or an analysis of style in the journal the student has been reading each week. The state-of-the-market article is a culminating assignment in that students are now aware of sources of information on employment opportunities, they have developed interviewing skills necessary to elicit answers to pertinent questions, and their experience in the course suggests a wider employment horizon than the one with which they entered the class. Here too, in an article accepted in lieu of a final examination, they have an opportunity to demonstrate improved style, mastery of appropriate tone, and all of the techniques they have been taught to use in enlivening their writing. Many select as their target publication either the Purdue student newspaper, the *Exponent*, or *The Graduate*, a national magazine tailored to an audience of graduating college seniors.

The analysis-of-style assignment requires an ability to assess tone, vocabulary, sentence and paragraph structure, and punctuation. It is not advised for the occasional student who instinctively writes well but cannot distinguish a subject from a verb, let alone a simple from a compound-complex sentence. This assignment, unlike the article on the state-of-the-job-market, has no target audience other than the class—mostly because the teacher has been unable to think of one.

WHY IT IS POPULAR

The course's popularity is, I believe, due to the opportunity it gives students to acquire skills within a context of assignments which simulate actual duties of people who earn their livings writing for science, government, industry, or education. That it is a practical course is attested by the number of former students now plying editorial skills in their jobs, as well as a recent graduate's letter describing a successful job interview:

> I found that the classwork I had done with various technical communications was quite beneficial. I was able to "talk shop" to a certain extent and I could answer specific questions concerning various types of publications—e.g., what is the purpose of in-house literature?
>
> . . . Several of my old class assignments formed the basis of a portfolio. And, although various class criticisms seemed petty at the time, incorporating such criticism into my work improved future assignments substantially.
>
> . . . One more thing—up until this past semester I had acquired a pretty good mish-mash of writing skills. But it was not until 515 that I could put them in order and apply them practically. . . .

Donald P. Rogers

Teaching Organizational Communication: Philosophy and Commitment

This article presents a justification for offering courses in organizational communication and considers strategies for designing a major/minor/concentration in organizational communication.

An undergraduate came to me and said, "I want a course that will prepare me for a job." I said, "Is that all?" The undergraduate said, "I want a program of study that will prepare me for a career." I said, "Is that all?" The undergraduate said, "I want an education that will prepare me for a life." I said, "Okay."

The above interchange illustrates the basic commponents of a student-centered rationale for offering organizational communication. In a large measure that rationale is, "Give the students what they want." It is an acceptable rationale, however, only when the student is behaving as an intelligent consumer of educational services. Specifically, in 1977, the job market is tight and many students are apprehensive about finding work. This is an understandable reaction to an unpleasant situation.

However, a great number of students are approaching the situation in a short-sighted manner. They demand immediate vocational training. In organizational communication (-type) courses they often get it. For example, one course in interviewing/technical writing, negotiating, copywriting, public relations. speech writing is often enough for the student to get a job as an interviewer/technical writer, etc. We can (and do and should) offer courses that give students marketable entry-level skills. The danger in doing so is that these kinds of jobs are deadend jobs. The student, of course, had the responsibility for intelligent consumption, but that doesn't absolve us. If we are going to offer vocational courses we must (like the bars) reserve the right to refuse service.

Obviously as educators we can't simply deny students access to certain courses, nor in times of declining enrollments do we want to. Our option is to include a warning, "CAUTION, the long term occupational opportunities in _______ are poor without additional training!" If students persist in ignoring the warning then stronger measures (prerequisites, linked courses, etc.) are needed.

JUSTIFICATIONS FOR THE OFFERINGS

Offering Vocational-type Organizational Communication Courses Prepares Students for Jobs

Of course, if we are going to include a warning advising additional training, we must be ready to offer courses that provide additional training. The key word in that sentence is "additional." Too often the reaction to the advice "offer more courses," is to offer more of the same. The student who takes four, five, six different courses which prepares him or her for four, five, six different entry-level jobs has a short-term advantage, but the same long-term disadvantage. He or she may simply have the option of choosing from among several deadend jobs.

Developing programs of study that will prepare students for careers in communication demands both effort and individualization. For example, it is fairly easy to enumerate the kinds of jobs available to an interviewer, but where do these jobs lead? We should encourage our students to look beyond the first job. This requires a certain amount of career planning—something that a student oriented towards the here and now may not understand. (Note: The question "What do you want to be doing in five years?" still perplexes students.) If the student decides to go into research, we may suggest a program of study that includes survey research, research methods, statistics, audience analysis, communication management, etc. The point is not that we should direct students, but that we should help them to find directions and then we should prepare them to proceed on their own.

Offering Career Counseling and Advanced Organizational Communication Courses Prepares Students for Careers

If someone were to implement the implicit advice of this discussion (up to now), the result would be a curriculum for educating specialists. Most departments do not have the resources to offer a number of career tracks and would be forced to concentrate. That is neither necessary nor desirable. Communication is a specialized field only at the entry level. The advanced courses in organizational communication can do multiple service.

For example, there is no reason for the typical department to offer multiple introductory research courses (Research in Organizational Communication, Research in Writing, Research in Public Relations, etc.). Offer one research course with built-in flexibility for the student to make individual applications. Despite student wishes for specialization and professionalization there is no good justification for narrow concentration on the undergraduate level. The most common complaint about students trained in areas that do specialize on the undergraduate level (e.g., engineering, accounting) is that they do not have the breadth of understanding to cope with constant and changing problems.

Offering General Communication Courses Prepares Students for Flexible Futures

The rationale for the undergraduate course in organizational communication developed so far has been strictly student centered, but there is another side that deserves mention. Many departments need to increase their enrollments; offering courses in organizational communication may be a way of tapping sources of students not otherwise available. A word of caution is important. Several universities have had the experience that the first time(s) O.C. courses are offered they attract from other department courses rather than from other departments or undecided majors. There is no guarantee that O.C. courses will increase total department enrollments (unless these courses are required by other departments).

Even without the lure of additional students there are some very good reasons for an instructor to offer courses in organizational communication. First, the area is relatively new, so fresh perspectives are welcome and the opportunity to make significant contributions is great. Second, the subject matter is important (relevant?). We are affected by the communication networks of our own organizations, the communication campaigns of other organizations, and the output of the communications industry. Third, the subject matter is interesting. Fourth, teaching is a good base for research in a wide-open area. Fifth, teaching is a good base for consulting. Sixth, perhaps most important, O.C. is a part of the wave of the future. It is a body of knowledge that is transdisciplinary in scope, method, and application. It is an area that holds great promise for contributing to the advancement of knowledge and possible unification of the behavioral sciences.

At this point it is fairly clear why someone might want to teach organizational communication, but not how someone goes about getting into the business. The next section of this paper deals with strategies for developing organizationa communication. Four types of straegries are considered: Recruitment, Instruction, Curriculum, and Placement.

STRATEGIES FOR DEVELOPMENT

Recruitment Strategies

In times of declining enrollments the recruitment of students can be a matter of life or death for a department. Courses in organizaational communication can be structured to meet the needs of other departments. The idea is to offer courses that other departments will require their students to take. The most likely candidates (based on expressions of need and past experience) are management; engineering and applied sciences; health sciences—especially nursing, occupational therapy, and hospital administration; educational administration; social sciences—especially clinical psychology, social work, and speech pathology; and physical education.

A second strategy is to determine if other departments are offering courses that they don't want to be offering; English often offers courses in business communication that they don't want; psychology and social work may not want to teach interviewing; speech or journalism often teach advertising because no one else will. The idea is that if another department has a course (or several) that your department would like to be teaching, find out if they would be willing to turn the course over to you.

A third strategy for recruiting students is simply to take out an ad in the local campus newspaper describing your course offerings. To some extent these recruitment strategies may be unnecessary. There are not that many areas of study which prepare B.A. students for jobs. Once word of a job/career major spreads, recruitment may not be a problem.

Instruction Strategies

The core element in any instructional strategy for organizational communication is the progressive movement away from the classroom as the learning environment. This same strategy fits both the single course and the multiple course program. A typical pattern would begin in the classroom moving from lecture to laboratory to case study to structured field experience to internship. Instruction in O.C. needs to blend theory with applications. The theory is the base from which the student may explore individualized interests. Applications of theory to problem situations may take place in the classroom laboratory as role-played asignments (conduct an interview, write a memo, etc.) or case study discussions (what would you do in the circumstances?). It is desirable, however, that instruction in O.C. not be confined to the classroom. In any community there are many opportunities to study organizational communication in action. Students can help local politicians with campaigns (writing press releases, writing speeches, interviewing voters). Students can analyze the organization, output, and impact of local media (radio, T.V., newspapers). Students can be the field agents in faculty originated research projects. Your own campus probably has a number of administrators charged with communication responsibilities, many of whom would be willing to accept student observers, shadows, interns for a term.

Curricular Strategies

The easiest tendency in an area like organizational communication is to to confuse a course with curriculum. Offering one course in O.C. gives the student an additional option within a department, but seldom prepares the student to meet job/career objectives. In general, however, it is not difficult to develop a curriculum in O.C. that relies on existing offerings. Students accepted into an O.C. major/minor (or whatever it's called) should have 1) a broad foundation in the liberal arts and humanties, 2) general knowledge of the applied social sciences (economics, management, government, education, etc.), and 3) specific courses in communication theory and behavior. The ideal curriculum in O.C. would involve four courses.

First, a basic introductory, survey, theory course to acquaint students with opportunities, directions, concepts, and principles of organizational communication, would be offered to sophomores or juniors. Second, one or more practicum courses should be offered to sophomores or juniors to develop specific skills in the spoken, print, and tele-communication media. This type of practicum course should not be too heavily weighted towards a single medium. For example, a presentations course in which the student prepares a written report, a presentation manuscript, audiovisual supporting materials, and finally delivers the oral report would be better than either the traditional public speaking or report writing course. Third, an applications course providing opportunities to observe organizations, to conduct field research, to analyze and discuss communication problems under the direction of a faculty supervisor to juniors or seniors. Fourth, internships should be made available for seniors to carry out independent observation, research, teaching, etc. These internships could be of any length from two weeks to a year.

Courses one and two may be taken concurrently. Courses one and two should be prerequisites for course three. Course three should be a prerequisite for course four. In the typical department there are probably existing courses that could fill the requirements of courses two and three. The only curricular changes that would be required in most cases would be the adoption of course one and four and some modification of existing courses to better meet the O.C. needs expressed in courses two and three.

Placement Strategies

In the long run placement may be the most important activity for the O.C. program. The first step in a comprehensive placement strategy is to make studens aware of job and career opportunities in communication. Most B.A. graduates take personal contact positions such as interviewers, counsellors, representatives, negotiators, recruiters, etc. in areas like Personnel, Public Relations, Customer Relations, Advertising, Labor Relations, Public Information, Marketing, Sales, Teaching, Training, etc. A smaller number take technical positions such as writers, editors, producers, or researchers in areas like Publishing, Broadcasting, or Internal Communication. Advancement tends to be into management, training, research, and consulting. Once aware, students should be encouraged to think about and plan their careers. This can be treated like the planning stage of a communication campaign.

Third, students should be taught how to write cover letters requesting interviews, how to write a resume, how to be interviewed, how to interview the interviewer, how to negotiate salary, travel, etc. All of this material can be integrated into courses in the second and fourth parts of the curriculum. Finally, beat the bushes for your students. Go to local recruiters, company personnel departments, placement agencies, communication organizations. Tell them to come to you when they are looking for employes because you have a continuing supply of well educated human beings. You will.

4

Grading Practices

Francis W. Weeks

The Meaning of Grades

Grades constitute a system of symbols. A grade symbol has no inherent meaning. It may have different meanings for the student, the teacher, the graduate school admissions officer, and an employer—since meanings are in people not in symbols. This paper tells what letter grades mean to one professor.

I once attended a meeting on the subject of the University's grading system and listened to all the arguments pro and con for changes in the system. I stayed after the meeting and talked to several students who were rather obviously upset by the discussion.

They were upset because so many of the faculty speakers dwelt on graduate school admission standards. The students protested (rightly, I think) that they didn't want to be graded on their potential as future graduate students.

But that raises the question, "What is the basis for grading?":

1. Promise as a future graduate student?
2. Promise as a future employee for a company?
3. Ability to beat out other students in a competition for grades?

All of these considerations came up during the discussion, and none of them pleased the students.

I came away believing that the honest and serious student wants a professional evaluation of his or her achievement. In some courses that achievement means mastery of subject content which presumably can be tested. In other courses it's the ability to solve problems. In still others it's the acquiring of a skill—such as writing.

What never came out during any of the discussions was the nature of grades as a symbol system. To us in Business Communication this should seem a most obvious and the most basic consideration. Those five letter grades A through E are a set of symbols. Each has no inherent meaning nor any reality in itself. Meanings that are attached to these symbols exist in the minds of the faculty, the students, and all those who use them for various purposes.

It should not be surprising, therefore, that a B in a course should have different meanings for the instructor, for the student, for the graduate school admissions officer, and for the company recruiter. Because of the great confusion about grading it seems that we have not been able to attach any long-lasting, generally-agreed-upon meanings to these symbols. I think the best definitions of grades are the ones written by Alta Gwinn Saunders in the 1920's and still used at Illinois:

A In addition to the qualities of a "B" paper, imagination, originality, and persuasiveness.

B Thorough analysis of the problem, a satisfactory solution, judgment and tact in the presentation of this solution, good organization, and an appropriate style of writing.

C Satisfactory analysis of the problem, organization, and writing style; but nothing remarkably good or bad about the paper.

D Presence of a glaring defect in a paper otherwise well done; or routine, inadequate treatment.

E Inadequate coverage of essential points, poor organization, offensive tone, careless handling of the mechanics of language.

You might discuss with your students the subject "Grades as a Symbol System." You could bring in references to Haney's *Communication and Organizational Behavior* because grades can provide a perfect example of the semantic phenomenon known as by-passing.

By simply going around the room and asking half a dozen students "What does an A mean to you?", "What does a B mean to you?", etc., you will discover that the students are in as much disagreement about the meaning of grades as the faculty.

At the end of the discussion you might have the courage then to say "When I give you an A, I am in effect saying this to you . . ." Then go on and describe exactly what it does mean to you . . . and the rest of the grades.

Of course, there are some students who will not want to take part in the discussion at all, claiming that all grades are meaningless and that all discussion is futile. In that case then, the student shouldn't care whether he gets a C, D, or E since none of the grades mean anything anyway. As soon as that possibility is suggested, he will probably quickly protest that although all grades are meaningless and he has no regard for them whatsoever, he still wants an A.

When I hold such a discussion with my students, I wind it up by telling them exactly what I communicate when I give final grades; namely:

1. If I give you an A for the course, that means I think very highly of you both in terms of your knowledge of communication, your ability to solve communication problems and to write very well. I would recommend you to anyone wanting to hire a person who is knowledgeable and skillful in communication. More than that, if I heard of a position requiring an unusually capable person in communications, I would probably get in touch with you and suggest that you apply for it.

2. If I give you a B in the course, that means that I think well of you, that you are reasonably knowledgeable and skillful, that you will never embarrass the University of Illinois by your performance after you leave here. I would write a recommendation for you for a position requiring communication skills, although it would not be couched in such glowing terms as it would be it you'd received an A in the course. I still stand behind you as one of my products, however.

3. If you get a C in the course, that means I think you are good enough in terms of knowledge, problem solving ability, and writing skill to get by. It means that I have not seen any evidence yet that you will distinguish yourself in this area, but that doesn't rule out the possibility that you will in the future. It also means that I know of no serious handicaps that you possess. I would rather, however, not write a recommendation for you.

4. I think we all agree that a D means a bare minimum to get by and carries no other favorable connotations.

5. E—I doubt very much that there will be any E's in the class (or even D's for that matter) since by the middle of the semester those who are not doing reasonably satisfactory work usually drop the course.

John Penrose

Students Grading Students—Worth Considering

Most college-level grading does not lend itself to participation by students; you, the instructor, are the expert and the students are naive participants. With the business communication in-class group audiovisual presentation, however, the students in the audience and the group members themselves can be centrally involved in the grading. This article describes a student self-grading system that the students appreciate, that appears to be fair and accurate, and over which the instructor maintains control.

As much as most of us may dislike it, evaluations of students are a fact of life. As teachers, we generally review the performances of our students and respond with letter or number grades. Grades on various assignments, presentations, or examinations are usually combined to determine a grade for the entire course. In most classes the students have little or no part to play in the evaluation of other students, and it is even more rare for undergraduates to be actively involved in any aspect of the grading system.

For most university-level courses, the omission of student evaluations is justified because the student is unfamiliar with the subject matter. It would be inappropriate, in other words, for a student in a chemistry class to grade a fellow classmate's performance on an experiment that is outside the evaluator's range of knowledge.

Business Communication is unusual in the college curriculum because the students, for the most part, are familiar with the topics *prior to* their entrance in the course. Our students may not possess expertise with each item, but they are readily aware of letters, reports, interpersonal speech communication, telephone usage, and conferences. This may not be true for the elementary psychology student confronted with stimulus-response paradigms, cognitive dissonance, reinforcement, or the semantic differential.

There can be benefits from student grading of other students: the students develop a feeling that it is "their course" and that they are an active part of it; they become aware that their feelings are respected; the recipients of the student-prepared grades often are quicker to accept them because of the peer-level origin; and the students gain some organized experience in that common business practice of evaluating others' performance.

In view of the general familiarity of the students with many of our topics and the possible benefits to be gained from student evaluations, I set about designing into my undergraduate course some of the more positive aspects of student grading. Of course the common arguments against any student grading had to be entertained: you, the instructor, are the expert; the students will be too lenient (or too strict) with each other; they do not yet possess the expertise to grade each other; or that they will not be consistent in their evaluations.

Within my course, of the several exams, short and report-length written assignments, and group oral presentations that make up the graded elements, the presentation was selected for student grading. This part of the course usually makes up 25 percent of the total grade. Although there were many reasons for the selection of this one and only element for the evaluations, the main ones were that it was felt a naive audience could evaluate a group's ability to meet the two criteria set forth for each presentation: their ability to present useful, relevant information, and to deliver it in an interesting fashion; and that a "leveling effect" would take place when an entire audience evaluated a group of five or six, rather than evaluating just one individual. Further, the six or seven presentations during the course allowed the audience to develop experience in evaluating without taking too much classroom time.

The determination of each individual's grade for the group presentation then was the product of three grading elements: the audience's evaluation, the group members' internal evaluations, and a review by the instructor.

Prior to the 30-minute presentation each member of the audience was given an anonymous form on which, both during and after the presentation, he could evaluate the group on such elements as clarity of information, teamwork, usefulness of information, group's understanding of information, and appropriate use of audiovisual aids. Grading was done with one of the five letter grades. The average letter grade from the audience became the "group grade."

Next, the instructor reviews the appropriateness of the audience's grade. This right-to-revise is "held in reserve" in case an audience seriously errs in its judgement. Although this method could be considered to work against the entire concept of student evaluations, it appears to be a necessary element. It is explained carefully to each class that information presented to them that appeared shallow, and was graded harshly, might actually be the result of extensive research and effort. As the "expert," the instructor should be able to adjust the group grade to reflect this. If appropriate then, the group grade is modified.

It is important to note that this right to modify group grades is seldom used, and when it is exercised, the change is usually not more than a third of a letter grade (e.g., "B" to "B-").

Finally, a confidential evaluation of each member of the group, including himself, was completed after the presentation by each group participant. Evaluations were made, by name, on such items as quantity and quality of assistance, and attendance at outside meetings. Data supplied on these forms have allowed the determination of those students doing more than their share as well as less than their share of the work. This information is used to move individual students away from the adjusted group score, as necessary.

This system has been in use for several years now, and appears to be successful. The students appreciate it. I feel the grading is appropriate. The frequent complaints of group work that, "I did more than my share of the work and got the same grade as everyone else," and "Joe did nothing and still got a good grade" are largely overcome. Analysis has shown a fairly wide dispersion of grades, and no favoritism for early versus late time locations over the one-month reporting period. The photocopied results (typed compilations of the audience's responses) that are distributed to each group member develop particularly keen interest.

If you haven't ventured into the "never-never" land of student evaluations, maybe these experiences will be of some assistance.

Caryl P. Freeman and Richard A. Hatch

A Behavioral Grading System that Works

The checkmark grading system applies behavioral principles of education and management to the problem of our mountains of student papers. It allows the teacher to be coach rather than judge in homework grading. Students learn better and like it better than under the regular letter grade or point systems, and the teacher can finish the job more quickly. Try it . . . you'll like it!

This is not your usual run-of-the-mill article touting a "better" way to do the same old job. Instead, it is a good old-fashioned, tub-thumping commercial. The fact is—we've finally found a GOOD way to grade homework!!! (Not the best of the bad ways, mind you, but a positively GOOD way!) And it's good from everyone's point of view:

—Teachers can take less time to look at more papers, be more honest about student writing, write far fewer comments, and set higher writing standards.

—Students finally have all the freedom they need to experiment and really LEARN to write—without fear of being marked down for experimenting.

—Even department chairs like the new student attitude about a compulsory course—and the new high grades that students are able to earn. (Yes, the word is EARN. Standards are just as high, but more students are meeting them!)

It all began when an experienced typing and shorthand teacher was assigned to teach a communications class. In typing and shorthand, students spend hours and hours practicing typing or taking dictation so they can develop enough proficiency to pass a test. The practice material that is good enough to meet test standards gets a checkmark. When a student collects enough checkmarks, he or she has earned the privilege of taking a test. Because the practice was well done, the student has confidence and usually does quite well on the test.

So, natuarally, the typing-teacher-turning-communication-instructor went to the same sort of system, reasoning that it was how well the student could write at the end of the semester that counted—not all the mistakes that he or she made in the process of learning. Future employers aren't interested in all the rotten practice; they want to know what the student can do for them.

The first informal experiment with this approach was so successful that in the Fall of 1972, a more formal experiment was conducted. Students in one section of Business Communication at Western Michigan University received the following handout at the beginning of the term:

GRADES

Your final grade for the course will be determined as follows: 40% determined by scores on two departmental exams; 60% determined by work on written assignments.

To determine your overall grade on the written assignments, use the following grade equivalents: A=15 or 16 acceptable papers; B=13 or 14 acceptable papers; C=11 or 12 acceptable papers; D=10 acceptable papers; E=fewer than 10 acceptable papers.

Each paper you hand in will be rated either "acceptable" (checkmark) or "needs revision" (no checkmark). [The checkmark was verbally defined as equivalent to B or better work.] Only checkmarked papers will be entered in the grade book. Noncheckmarked papers may be revised and resubmitted within a reasonable length of time; a checkmark on a paper that has been revised will count just as much as a checkmark on a first try. You may revise and resubmit a paper as many times as necessary, though I may ask you to hand in an alternative assignment rather than making some obvious (and thus not very useful) revisions in the original assignment.

A total of 16 assignments will be available for you to work on by the end of the semester. In addition, I will provide one makeup or alternative assignment, which you may do instead of one of the regular assignments.

I will use the following signals in commenting on your papers in addition to occasional full notes: !—Right on the nose! Great! I agree! Good thinking!; ?—What's this? Surely you didn't intend this? Please reconsider?; No!—Please find some way to eliminate this problem!

Most of the time, people seem to have little difficulty figuring out what these signals are meant to suggest. Occasionally you may find the signals puzzling—*please* check with me if you're in doubt about what the signal is supposed to suggest to you.

Because it was an experimental system, a brief questionnaire was administered to the 23 students who saw fit to attend class on the last day before mid-term vacation. The same questionnaire was again formally given to all students at the end of the semester. The responses are summarized in the following tables:

	Number of Responses	
	Mid-Term	End of Course
Now that you have had a chance to see how the checkmark system works, if you could go back to the beginning of the semester and choose between the checkmark system and the standard grade system, would you:		
Choose the checkmark system?	23	36
Not particularly care which system is used?	—	1
Choose the standard grading system?	—	—
Do you feel that your writing is improving? Can you write better now than you could at the beginning of the course?		
Yes	23	35
No	—	2
Do you feel that your writing assignments are being or have been evaluated fairly?		
Yes	23	36
No	—	1

Students were also asked for any comments on the system. There were NO negative comments (some did not comment at all). Among the favorable, the following seem to most clearly express some of the benefits of the system from the students' point of view:

"[The checkmark system] lets a student prove to himself that he can write a good letter or communicate an idea, even if it takes more than one try."

"The checkmark system is great because you keep doing it till you see what a good letter should look like in your own words, not someone else's!"

"Although I only have one checkmark (at mid-term), I can see where I made my mistakes, and maybe after ten times on the same paper I'll finally get a checkmark. I feel that if I were assigned to write a letter of the same kind, I would do a pretty good job."

"The checkmark system gives the student a chance for a good grade and also a chance to earn the grade."

"With the standard grading system, once you're shot down, you're shot down. With the checkmark system, there's a chance for constructive improvement."

"You can learn a heck of a lot more by seeing your mistakes and correcting them. If you just got back the paper, you wouldn't bother to rewrite it."

"You keep trying even if you don't do well the first time."

"Pressure is off with the checkmark system. We can experiment, but if the experiment is no good, rewrite the letter with no penalty."

"I think a teacher can make a wiser decision between assigning a check or no check than choosing between five letter grades."

From the students' comments, it is fairly clear that they like the system because it does provide a true opportunity to LEARN. It is, in fact, the ONLY system which completely meets the essential conditions for skill learning on which learning theorists now agree:

1. The student's goal is immediately and clearly defined.
2. Every correct or desirable response made by the student as he or she attempts to reach the goal is rewarded (reinforced).
3. Every incorrect or undesirable response made by the student as he or she attempts to reach the goal is either: a) Corrected (thereby becoming desirable and rewarded), or b) Ignored (to be crowded out by an increasing number of correct responses).

Systems of assigning grades or percents or points or whatever do not meet these essential conditions for learning.

The discussion below summarizes some of the important differences:

Student's Goal

Grading System: Get the assignment in and hope to pass. A "pass" is pretty indefinite, and the poor students can always console themselves that they will do better next time.

Checkmark System: Get an acceptable assignment in because otherwise it will have to be done over (and over . . . and over . . .)

Student's Rewards

Grading System: Only A papers are truly rewarded. The teacher's cheery comment, "Your first paragraph is fine, but . . ." is lost when the grade is less than A because the good is downgraded along with the bad.

Checkmark System: Good work does not need to be rewritten. The student has personal concrete evidence of what is "acceptable" writing. He or she is rewarded by not having to rewrite parts of the paper.

Corrections

Grading System: The teacher (who does NOT need the practice) does all the corrections and writes a small book—partly as correction and partly to justify the grade.

Checkmark System: The student (who DOES need the practice) does the rewriting with minimum suggestions from the teacher. There is a strong incentive to do a job, for otherwise it will have to be done again (and again . . . and again . . .)

Best of all, students are forced to write better and better until they can write well. Under a grading system, students may opt to pass the course by writing 15 or 16 C papers. They cannot do that with the checkmark system; they MUST write at least 10 GOOD papers to pass the course at all. They MUST demonstrate to themselves that they can write well, even if they decide to do the minimum work necessary to pass. At the very worst they have succeeded in learning enough to write 10 good papers.

This is the key difference between this system and the "contract" learning systems currently popular. This system is very similar to many of the contract systems, except that here students are not permitted to contract for mediocrity. They cannot contract to do C work. They must, in effect, contract to do at least a minimum amount of GOOD work to pass the course.

It's interesting that the approach suggested by the learning theorists (above) is paralleled in the growing literature on supportive management. McGregor's Theory Y, for example, is quite parallel. Blake and Mouton are saying (*The Managerial Grid*, Houston: Gulf Publishing Company, 1964, pp. 148-149): ". . . what mistakes do occur, the basic orientation of the manager is an educational one. He might say for example, 'Tough luck. It's embarrassing, but the thing is to study the problem and to learn from it. When can we get together?' "In other words, . . . discover the *cause* of the problem not just identify and punish the person associated with its occurrence." That is, don't just grade them down for doing it wrong; teach them how to do it right!

The best evidence that the system works can be seen in the following comparative summary. This table compares the outcome of the experimental checkmark grading with the outcome of a semester under the old standard grading system for the same instructor. As far as it is possible to maintain stable standards of evaulation, *the standards did not change* between these semesters; a checkmark in the experimental semester was in fact very much equivalent to a B grade (not including B-) in the previous semester. No wonder teachers love the system!

COMPARISON OF OUTCOMES UNDER CHECKMARK GRADING SYSTEM AND STANDARD GRADING SYSTEM

Number of Acceptable Papers Submitted by Student	Checkmark System* Acceptable = Checkmark	Standard System* Acceptable = B or Better
16	2	—
15	26	—
4	3	—
13	4	—
12	—	—
11	1	—
10	3	3
9	—	3
8	1	3
7	—	4
6	—	12
5	—	11
4	—	6
3	—	8
2	—	6
1	—	6
0	—	3
	40	65

*Total assignments: Checkmark system—16. Standard system—14.

Grade	Number of Students			
	Checkmark System		Standard System	
	Writing	Course	Writing	Course
A	28	20	6	12
B	7	14	41	29
C	1	1	17	21
D	3	4	1	2
E	1	1	0	1
	40 students		65 students	

But, you say, what about the poor teacher buried under a veritable avalanche of rewrites to grade? Strangely, there were not as many extra papers as might be expected.

NUMBER OF PAPERS SUBMITTED UNDER CHECKMARK SYSTEM AND STANDARD GRADING SYSTEM

Number of papers instructor would have graded under standard grading system (16 assignments x 40 students) 640

Number of papers actually submitted for evaluation under checkmark system. 904

Even though the standards of evaluation did not change, only one paper in two had to be rewritten. Why?

1. The most important reason is pure basic psychology. When a student turns in a paper to be graded, he or she is through with it. The rest of the job is on the teacher ("Ha, Ha—I wrote it during the break before class!"). But in the checkmark system, a mediocre paper will have to be rewritten, and the students know it. They quickly figure out that it's not rational to make extra work for themselves. Having to do the paper all over again the next day is a much more impressive motivator than the risk of a poor course grade two months away!

2. Of course, some students just never did get around to rewriting all the papers (see course outcome above).

3. The instructor can say—and mean, "For these first four papers, I will MARK all the problem areas. Beginning with paper five, any of these problems will cause you to rewrite the papers. But for now, you get a checkmark if you have successfully dealt with the spirit of the assignment and if you have done just this and this and this successfully." This allows us an honest and honorable way to provide some stepped learning experiences

for the student on these early assignments and to give the student some early successes. They don't get hit with the usual depressing deluge of learning necessary to complete that first assignment successfully. In the final analysis, the best way to make some kinds of errors go away may be to ignore them completely.

Still, you say, 904 papers are 904 papers—and I have four sections of papers to grade, not just one! Have no fear. It isn't really going to take you any longer, and it is a lot happier work. Some reasons:

1. It is fast work to skim through a stack of papers and sort them into only two piles—"Probably acceptable" and "definitely needs more work." The acceptable papers get a checkmark and a few exclamation points; you don't even have to take the time to write "Good," because success is its own reward. (Yes, really, it is!) The poor papers will have a few !'s (very easy to write and very important to the student), a ? or two, and some part that is circled and labeled "No!" That's all. You don't have to write a book on every paper, or take off 2 points for each misplaced comma.

2. When you don't have to assign a grade (or points or whatever) to every paper, you don't have to spend time on each paper justifying why the grade is not an A. Our grades are subjective; instructors and students understand that. However, if the student can look at his returned paper and be saying "How can I make this into a checkmark paper?" (instead of "Why isn't this an A paper?"), then our comments can actually be the constructive suggestions we want to write instead of the justifications we usually find ourselves writing. The student who knows he or she can rewrite the paper for full credit is in a position to receive constructive suggestions and doesn't need to be looking for justification.

3. You can stop feeling like such a pious hypocrite, writing, "This is one of the best papers you have written all year. Unfortunately, there are still so many problems (I hope you can read this through the glare of red marks) that I still couldn't grade you higher that a D+. But keep trying. I'm sure you'll do better next time." You might have fooled yourself, but you never fooled the student for a minute. He or she always hated you for going out of your way to write some nice dumb platitude about a stupid D paper. You don't know what freedom is until you can write in the middle of the term, "This is AWFUL—you better

start over from scratch," and have the student accept that honestly. In the meantime, everyone's emphasis has changed from "avoiding the bad" to "trying for GOOD."

4. Gone, too, are the days of keeping track of who turned what in on time, or how late. You'll never be able to keep track of what's on time and what's not, and of course that's never been the point anyway. The question is, "What can the student do *at the end of the semester?*"

5. Best of all is your own new attitude. Finally, you have a chance to do what you came into teaching for—helping others to improve—instead of spending your time judging exactly how bad your students are and watching them get worse.

Some suggestions on setting up your own experiment:

1. This system appears to work well in any course where there are repetitive skill-building opportunities. If your course has more than 10 or 12 assignments of more-or-less equal weight during the semester, then simply adapt your grade-equivalent standards from the set suggested above. If your course has only half a dozen assignments in a semester, you'll probably need to do some serious adapting to make this system work.

2. In setting your grade-equivalent standards (how many checkmarks make an A, etc.), take the viewpoint of a student rationally working for a grade. A passing grade in the course should require that the student do more than half of the work acceptably, possibly much more than half. The D range (and perhaps the C range) should be small—"Why should I settle for a D, when I can do only one more paper acceptably and get a C?" (What simpler way is there to get the student to practice just a little more?) There's no point in letting the A range be larger than one assignment; if the student can get his A for doing 15 assignments accepably and gets no more credit for doing the 16th assignment, why should he or she do it? (Look at the table; in our experimental section, only two did that last assignment.)

3. Set the total number of assignments at least as high as you usually set it in that course, perhaps a bit higher. Give yourself clear proof that the system works!

4. Explain the new system to the students right at the beginning of the semester, and tell them frankly that you are experimenting. Let them know why you think the system is better, and make it clear that if the system doesn't work, you'll go back to the old system with no possible loss to them. This will help you

retain their sympathy as you make the first few mistakes in getting the kinks out of your way of applying the system.

A final word: At Western Michigan University this semester, we are trying the method in other sections with other teachers and adapting the basic principles to fit other types of courses (including, for example, a Freshman English course). The results so far are every bit as good as in the first experimental section.

Quite honestly, it took a lot of nerve to commit a class to the system the first time. It IS a huge departure from everthing we've always done in communication courses. For years we've spent hours commiserating and hashing over the paper-grading problem and how to lighten the load. But it still is a GIANT step into the unknown actually to take the lid off completely and say, "I'll avoid the grading problem once and for all by simply not grading—just demanding good work."

We can promise it works, now; but a year ago we were starting our own little experiment in fear and hope. You go ahead and try one section—your world won't grind to a halt because of just one little experiment. Once you have tried the checkmark system, we practically guarantee you'll never go back to any other system of handling homework.

Try it . . . you'll like it!

David P. Throop and Daphne A. Jameson

Behavioral Grading: An Approach Worth Trying

Because a behavioral grading system produces exciting results, more writing teachers should try it. With slight modifications, they can adapt it to their own programs. In the experiment reported here, anticipated problems failed to materialize; grading took no more time; conferences were positive, productive experiences; all students could write checkmark-quality papers; final grades were not inflated; and the extra class time allowed more exercises and workshops. The behavioral grading system helps the student learn to revise, an important skill rarely taught. The system makes the classroom atmosphere positive and cooperative since students and teacher work together to achieve success with minimum rewriting. The adversary relationship between teacher and student disappears. Consequently, most students learn more with this system than with a traditional one.

Perhaps the best technique for teaching writing was the one which Flaubert supposedly used with the young Maupassant. As the story goes, Flaubert was an established man of letters when the fledgling Maupassant approached him for help. Each Sunday, as Flaubert finished lunch and lingered over his coffee, Maupassant would be admitted to the older gentleman's chambers and would hand over another story. Flaubert would read the story carefully, sip his coffee thoughtfully, and having finished both would lean over to the fireplace and drop the story into the flames. All without a word. This ritual was continued over a period of many months. Each Sunday another effort would be reduced to ashes. But one day Flaubert did not discard the story; instead, he handed the manuscript to Maupassant and said simply, "Publish it." Maupassant did submit it for publication, it was accepted, and his career was launched.

Unfortunately, not all of us have the stature and critical confidence of Flaubert. And some of our students might complain if we employed his technique. Until some magic wand is marketed which can ensure instant excellence in our students, we all must keep searching for methods and approaches which can increase the possibility of success.

When Caryl Freeman and Richard Hatch made their enthusiastic pitch for a behavioral grading system in the June 1975 *Bulletin*, we reacted with mixed emotions. Certainly any method was worth trying that offered a reduction of frustration for both students and teachers and that increased the chances for genuinely successful student writing. The real question, however, was whether this method could really work for us.

We believed ourselves to be tough-minded evaluators who expected high-quality work (which we all too seldom received). Could our students actually perform quality work on a consistent basis? Since we believed that students learn to write by writing, we already maintained as demanding an assignment level as prudence and reason allowed. With the same number of assignments (sixteen graded papers plus an equal number of ungraded classroom exercises in a fifteen-week semester), would our students have the time or energy needed for revision, and would we be able to cope with the increased number of papers? Most of all, we feared being manuevered into giving a larger number of A's and B's, which would reflect neither the students' real abilities nor performance.

Frankly, we were amazed.

Performance levels were genuinely higher. In fact, our opinion of the average student's ability has changed significantly.

Yes, the paper load increased appreciably. But, using the decreased number of comments suggested by Freeman and Hatch, we spent LESS time grading papers over the semesters.

And yes, grades did rise. But not excessively. And students earned those higher grades.

So this article is a success story. We agree that this past semester with the behavioral grading system was the most rewarding and least frustrating of any we have experienced. Behavioral grading is not a panacea or a magic wand, but it is very adaptable; it can work for a wide range of people in the large spectrum of writing courses. We'd like to show you some of the modifications we made and discuss some positive benefits you might not have considered.

HOW TO MINIMIZE ANTICIPATED PROBLEMS

No system is perfect, but most of the problem areas we anticipated or encountered with this one simply did not interfere appreciably with the learning process.

Excessive Time Grading Papers

Together, we had a 49 percent increase in the total number of papers. But these papers were graded much more quickly. Particularly in the second half of the semester most students were performing well, and our comments, even on unsatisfactory efforts, were relatively minimal. While we never reached the point of comfort with the three recommended symbols, we were able to limit comments to general problem areas, especially with revisions (i.e., "opening para lacks coherence" or "better you-att needed throughout"). We were able to diagnose problems without prescribing specific remedies and to focus on improvements without listing shortcomings.

To prevent having to grade a huge stack of papers at the end of the semester, we required that students submit rewrites within one week of receiving papers back. This deadline plan effectively prevented backlog.

Endless Conferences

Naturally, this approach encourages students to come in to discuss things they don't understand. So the time gained from grading papers was applied to individual discussions. But we much preferred talking with students rather than writing at them. And the conferences were effective, since the emphasis was entirely on writing improvement with few arguments about grades. The number of students coming in decreased toward the latter part of the semester as fewer students needed our assistance or condolences.

Chronic Mediocrity

Since this system requires B-level performance on a majority of assignments, we were concerned that some students would never achieve a legitimate checked paper. But students who in previous semesters might have been written off as mediocre, beginning with C's and finishing with C+'s, were able to perform well and seemed genuinely excited about it. Occasionally we may have stretched the checkmark to include a C+, but not often. Most students can do positively good work, especially if they see little alternative. Even students on the pass-fail option soon realized they had to do some good work, just to pass.

Misrepresentation of Students' Ability/Performance

We were bothered by the new bugaboo, grade inflation. However, we were able to control the numbers instead of allowing the numbers to control us. In-class papers may be counted among the checks, but without allowing revision. Or they may be graded with the standard A-B-C-D-E method. The rationale for this is both simple and straightforward. Unlimited revisions are designed to improve the quality of writing and thinking, not simply to achieve success in a given assignment. Therefore, if the accumulated checkmarks represent improvement, students should expect to do well on an in-class assignment.

In fairness to the student, and as an allowance for those who are improving slowly, most of these graded in-class assignments should be given in the latter part of the semester when most have had ample opportunity to master the principles and develop their style. Another way to offset an unrealistically high number of checkmarked papers is to weight the examinations more heavily than usual. To justify this, the examinations should require writing, whether problems, essays, or short answers, and should be evaluated for both writing style and objective content.

Limited Classroom Activities

We had spent a great deal of class time in previous semesters going over problems, evaluating student solutions using transparencies and handouts, and generally telling our classes where most of them had gone wrong. Under the behavioral grading system, we couldn't present solutions to each assignment since many in the class had not yet completed it satisfactorily. Students had to rely upon their ingenuity and effort to solve each problem. And the shining example of excellence for each problem was ultimately their own.

They saw good solutions that used their ideas and were written in their very own style. With extra class time available, we were able to use many more exercises, sentence and paragraph drills, and miniproblems designed to develop quick analysis. We found less need for lecturing. We sometimes held workshops during scheduled class time with optional attendance where students could come in with works in progress, past assignments still needing revision, or simply ideas they wanted to talk about. The informality was both refreshing and effective.

HOW THE SYSTEM SUCCEEDS

Some of the positive benefits of behavioral grading were unanticipated but very gratifying.

Students Learn to Revise

Revising is an important skill too often neglected in writing classes. Most of the time, when we insist upon revision, students simply respond directly to our specific criticisms without thinking much. They seem to believe that if a sentence isn't marked up, then it must be good. At the same time, if we bury the paper under an avalanche of red marks (or green or purple), students can become depressed and despairing. With behavioral grading, they have to think and plan for improvements. Most students learned the difference between a first draft and a finished copy. The workshops were particularly useful for tearing apart first drafts in a constructive team effort.

Creativity Encouraged

Much as we pay lip service to creativity, most students, with their self-preservation instincts fully operative, will choose the safe and bland solution. They won't take chances when a grade is involved, but they will take chances when they know an unsuccessful (but often interesting) effort can be revised without penalty.

Defensive Grading Eliminated

We spent less time grading papers during the semester, but more importantly, we did not have to grade defensively. How many teacher's comments only serve to justify why a paper is a D+ rather than a C-? How many conferences have bogged down in a tense confrontation over the almighty grade? But now students will believe you when you tell them you are on their side because they know you don't want to read extra revisions any more than they wish to write them. The atmosphere becomes more purposeful, with a mutual "let US get this problem resolved" attitude.

Student Attitudes Improved

In this program students believe they can control their own fate in the classroom, and they are right. With the teacher establishing certain minimum standards, the student believes he can aim for his own personal goals and reasonably expect to achieve them. How many students have we lost by the fourth or fifth week of the semester? They sit somewhere in the back of the classroom, convinced that a C or a D is all they can expect no matter what they do. So they do little and justify their pessimistic expectations. But no longer. Our students believed they could do well, or at least improve, throughout the semester.

On questionnaires given during the eighth week of the semester, 91 percent of the students favored the new grading system. By the end of the semester 95 percent indicated that preference. During the last week of the semester, 98 of the students said their writing had improved or was still improving, and 91 percent believed their papers had been judged fairly. This optimism reflected itself in both the quantity and the quality of the work produced. We may be waving the carrot before the donkey with this approach, but the carrot does lure them on to their best efforts. Not all students are excellent, but if they perform to the best of their individual abilities, they have succeeded and so have we.

WHY THE SYSTEM WORKS

We identified three factors which give this system great credibility. First, we give our students constant and positive reinforcement. By mutual agreement, student and teacher choose to ignore or forget unsuccessful efforts. Our focus is on success whether it comes today, tomorrow, or on the last day of class. But when success does arrive, it is welcomed without reservation.

Second, we can reduce the students' ego-involvement in writing. No matter how much the teacher may rationalize, criticisms on a paper or grades less than an "A" are negative reinforcements. By eliminating the adversary relationship and inculcating a genuine team effort between student and teacher, we can drastically minimize this effect.

Finally, and most importantly, this system allows us to use basic student instincts to work for and not against our efforts. Most students wish to excel or at least be certified as excellent in the academy, preferably with as little effort as possible. Failing this, most students would like to place the onus on the teacher rather than on themselves. But under this behavioral grading system, students recognize that they can do as well as their abilities and efforts warrant. The teacher becomes supportive rather than destructive. The burden is clearly and inescapably upon the students' shoulders.

We want other people to try this system because we believe they would share our success. If you already have an approach which works well for you, then file this article. Some long day hence when things aren't working, you might want to try it. We are all looking for a method we're comfortable with, one which will enable us to help our students in the best ways possible.

Teaching writing is something like coaching football—always subject to innovations. The first year Texas installed the Wishbone (a run-oriented offense that objures the pass almost totally), Darrell Royal was asked if his team would throw in the Cotton Bowl. Responded Darrell, "We're going to dance with who brung us." This behavioral grading system has brought us a long way and we'll dance with it until something better comes along.

Joseph F. Ceccio

Checkmark Grading and the Quarter System

Are you still searching for a better way to handle student papers? This article can help you solve your problem. "Checkmark Grading and the Quarter System" provides a useful model, especially for those who teach a one-quarter course in Business Writing. Discussion focuses on four refinements of the original behavioral grading system and specific student reactions to the author's classroom experiment.

"The checkmark grading system is better than the standard grading system. The average student has a better chance of passing the course. His writing will also improve. The chance to revise his papers enhances his learning of the material. I'm glad that we're using this system. I'd like to see it used in my other courses."

"The checkmark system removes the strain and pressure from this class that would otherwise be there with the usual grading system. I can be creative without worrying about failing on a paper. If I have done something drastically wrong, instead of getting an "F" on the paper, I can resubmit it for a checkmark. I am doing better in this course than I expected, probably becasue of this new grading system, and I feel that I have accomplished a great deal this quarter."

—Two Wright State University
Business Writing Students

Last summer, as I was preparing to move from the University of Illinois to Wright State University in Dayton, a funny thing happened to me on the way to my new assignment: I read the Freeman-Hatch report on "A Behavioral Grading System That

Works," in *The ABCA Bulletin.* Theirs truly was a seminal article.

For several years, I, too, had been searching for a better way to handle student papers; the traditional, one-shot method of "you make the mistakes and I'll correct them" simply was *not* working any longer. The brilliance of the Freeman-Hatch system, as I saw it, was that it cut through all the destructive and depressing red tape of older grading techniques for *both* students and teachers alike. But would it work for me?

During July I began to rethink and revise my junior-senior Business Writing course in light of this new approach. I had to remember 1) that my classes were required for all students in the College of Business and 2) that Wright State followed the ten-week quarter schedule. By September I was ready to try out my own version of checkmark grading. The results? Even better than expected! The course became popular; the students prospered; they both learned and earned. And their teacher arrived at the same conclusion that Professors Freeman and Hatch had: "Once you have tried the checkmark system . . . you'll never go back to any other system of handling homework."[1]

FROM SEMESTER TO QUARTER: FOUR REFINEMENTS

With the help of the checkmark system, I turned a "required" course into an enjoyable and fruitful learning experience for most of the participants. My own adaptation involves four important refinements and could prove a useful model for those who teach a one-quarter course in Business Writing.

First, it was necessary to revise the grade equivalents. On the first day, the students were told that their final grade would be determined as follows:

25%—final exam on major terms and concepts and on a negative problem to solve; of less weight within this 25 percent are the five-minute oral critique, participation, and class contributions.

75%—work on written out-of-class assignments (Nos. 1-11).

My grade equivalents for the 75 percent worked well, and while the grade equivalents seemed fair to most students, the course was by no means a "pushover."

The introduction of three "Clearance Dates" was my second and most significant alteration in the original behavioral grading system. I heartily agreed with Freeman and Hatch that "The question is, 'What can the student do *at the end of the semester?*'"[2] ; but I could not see how that goal could be realistically achieved by permitting students to turn in nothing until the last week of classes, if they wished. A bit more structure seemed necessary.

In describing how papers would be handled, I explained to the class that we would have three Clearance Dates: one at the conclusion of week 4 for papers 1-4, one at the conclusion of week 7 for papers 5-8, and one at the conclusion of week 10 for papers 9-11. A Clearance Date, therefore, was the last day to turn in one or all of a certain group of papers—whether new or revised. After that date, we had to move on to other work. My course plan was deliberately set up so that each new problem was somewhat more complex or difficult than the one before it. I always advised my students to submit their papers the next class meeting after they were assigned, for in this way they would have plenty of time to revise and not be caught short with only a few acceptable papers at the end, and thus a lower grade for the 75 percent than they would like.

True, I have reduced some of the freedom in the original Freeman-Hatch plan, but many students actually appreciated these three Clearance Dates "limits" as ways to lay out and budget their own time better. I would hesitate to take advantage of checkmark grading without some such mechanism for helping students keep to a reasonable schedule.

Third, I thought that students needed to know more precisely (not just "verbally"[3]) the meaning of grades where a checkmark is "B" or better work, and so I provided them with clear (though not infallible) grade definitions drawn from *Business Writing Cases and Problems:*

A—In addition to the qualities of a "B" paper, imagination, originality, and persuasiveness.

B—Thorough analysis of the problem, a satisfactory solution, judgment and tact in the presentation of this solution, good organization, and an appropriate style of writing.

C—Satisfactory analysis of the problem, organization, and writing style; but nothing remarkably good or bad about the paper.

D—Presence of a glaring defect in a paper otherwise well done; or routine, inadequate treatment.

F—Inadequate coverage of essential points, poor organization, offensive tone, careless handling of the mechanics of language.[4]

The advantage of listing and describing the letter grades early in the course, even though we *weren't* putting them on the eleven papers, is fairly obvious. Students quickly realized that a check-mark was not an average grade (C) and that "acceptable" meant "demonstrating those qualities which we normally associate with A or B work."

My last refinement was to utilize a few more grading "signals" than "!" and "?" and "No!" I wanted, of course, to keep full annotation to a minimum, yet I needed some kind of shorthand to help students more readily see their problem areas. Menning and Wilkinson's "Concise Writer's Handbook" (Appendix D of *Communicating Through Letters and Reports*, the text for my course) filled the bill perfectly.[5] Students could now pinpoint their specific weaknesses, but I still didn't have to get bogged down in lengthy explanatory discussions. The abbreviated symbols which appeared most frequently included Adapt, Agr, CSP, Dev, Jar, Neg, Pas, PD, SC, and YA. Anyone who has taught from Menning and Wilkinson knows how efficient such symbols can be. Most comprehensive business communication texts provide a similar set of abbreviations for teachers and students.

In short, these four modifications or additions—the revised grade equivalents, the three Clearance Dates, the specific definitions for A-F, and the brief handbook symbols—provided a very effective means of grading the eleven written assignments (worth 75 percent) summarized below:

4—A-plan messages

2—Resume; Letter of Application

1—Memo Report (about 3 pages)

1—Library-researched Business Report (Taught jointly by a Library instructor and the course instructor; required for all students) on assigned topic or student's own topic.

2—C-plan messages

1—B-plan message

SPECIFIC STUDENT REACTIONS: FALL 1975

The two student comments with which this article began were quoted from the questionnaire I administered to two Business Writing classes (of approximately 22 students each) very late in the quarter. The reactions and responses, represented by the following table, are every bit as encouraging as the Freeman-Hatch experiment—even with my four refinements:

	Number of Responses	
	Class No. 1	Class No. 2
Now that you have had a chance to see how the checkmark system works, if you could go back to the beginning of the quarter and choose between the checkmark system and the standard grade system, would you:		
Choose the checkmark system?	17	15
Not particularly care which system is used?	—	3
Choose the standard grading system?	1	1
Do you feel that your writing is improving? Can you write better now than you could at the beginning of the course?		
Yes	16	17
No	2	2
Do you feel that your writing assignments are being or have been evaluated fairly?		
Yes	17	17
No	1	2

Finally, when asked to write down any comments they had on this system, to discuss benefits and disadvantages, most students wrote strongly in favor of my retaining the checkmark system in future quarters:

> "The checkmark system forces me to be more careful in my writing. With the standard grading system, I would probably turn in my first draft, whereas with the checkmark system I usually revise my papers several times. I believe I learn more with this new system."
>
> "A *very fair* means of evaluation, about the best I've seen at Wright State. Emphasis is rightly on discipline and dedication."

"Writing 11 papers under the usual grading system would be terrible! I like this system where you have a chance to do as well as you want to do. Since I am taking 5 other courses, I like the flexible due dates. I can devote sufficient time to papers and not just rush to hand something in on time."

"I like the responsibility and the leeway that the checkmark method gives the student."

"A possible disadvantage—a checkmark doesn't do as much for the ego as an A on a paper that required much thought and work."

"The checkmark system relieves much of the pressure to get an A or B that is present in the standard grading system. The student is able to concentrate on the effectiveness of the paper rather than on just trying to get a good grade."

"I do like the checkmark system since in the business world your written message will be either acceptable or unacceptable, not A, B, C, etc."

Well, I'm sold, as are most of the Wright State Business Students I've taught so far. I know that my students have been successful and that they have had to work hard for that success. Now . . . about that Freshman Composition course and the checkmark system . . . .

NOTES AND REFERENCES

1. Caryl P. Freeman and Richard A. Hatch, "A Behavioral Grading System That Works," *The ABCA Bulletin*, Vol. 38, No. 2, June 1975, p. 9.

2. Freeman and Hatch, p. 8.

3. Freeman and Hatch, p. 2.

4. Francis W. Weeks and Richard A. Hatch, *Business Writing Cases and Problems*, Champaign, IL: Stipes Publishing Company, 1974, p. iv.

5. See J. H. Menning and C. W. Wilkinson, *Communicating Through Letters and Reports*, Homewood, IL: Richard Irwin, 1972, pp. 692-733.

Barron Wells

A Plan for Grading Formal Business Reports

The task of grading a large number of lengthy reports is never a pleasant one for a teacher, and the prospect of having a large part of their grade depend on one paper is somewhat traumatic for most students. Any delay in returning the report to the student destroys the value of immediate feedback, and seldom does the student get to apply what can be learned from the teacher's evaluation of the report when it finally is returned. This article presents a plan for completing the report in several parts that helps to overcome some of these problems, as well as allows the report to be used as a teaching tool.

One complaint voiced by many teachers of Business Report Writing, whether as a separate course or as a part of a broader communication course, is that of having a large number of reports turned in to them at one time to be graded. This poses a seemingly overwhelming task for the teacher, and if the reports cannot be returned to the students promptly, the value of immediate feedback is lost.

Students also dislike the prospect of having a large portion of their course grade depend on a single grade on one report in some sort of "live-or-die, sink-or-swim" fashion. Often the student never gets a chance to apply what he learns from the teacher's marks on his report. In order to overcome some of these problems, I handle the longer, formal report in my report writing classes in the following manner:

1. The report is divided into five essential components: a) an introduction giving a background and description of the problem to be solved, the purpose of the report, etc.; b) a review of the procedures used in collecting data for the report; c) the secondary data pertaining to the topic; d) the primary data pertaining to the topic; and e) the summary, conclusions, and recommendations.

2. A large part of the course content is organized around the five components outlined above.

3. As each component is covered in class, students complete the corresponding part of their report and submit it to be evaluated and graded.

4. After each of the five components of the report have been returned, students make all corrections that have been indicated and re-submit the complete report. A title page, table of contents, bibliography, and appendix are added at this point.

This system does not reduce the total amount of work done by the teacher; in fact, it may seem to add more work, because each student's work is submitted to the teacher twice. However, it does distribute the work load more evenly throughout the semester. Also, when the complete report is submitted (step 4 above), it need only be evaluated to whatever extent the teacher feels is necessary. It may be necessary only to check to see that corrections have been made, to check the new parts (title page, etc.), and to check for consistency from one component to another; something that is not feasible when the components are being submitted individually.

More important, the student benefits in several ways. First, the student gets an opportunity to reinforce proper procedures by correcting initial errors and re-doing the report. Second, the student gets quicker feedback and an opportunity to improve before the entire report is submitted. Third, the grade for this part of the course is divided over six assignments and does not depend entirely on any one submission.

While this system does not solve all the problems of the report writing teacher or the students, it can help considerably.

A final comment about the teaching of Business Report Writing seems in order. Those of us who have survived such things as research papers in graduate courses, master's theses, and doctoral dissertations tend to be oriented toward the academic-type of formal paper, which carries over too much into our classes. Surprisingly, most of our textbooks also seem to have this same orientation to a large extent. In actual business situations, however, very few reports are organized and presented in the traditional academic format. Care should be exercised in our Business Communication courses to give adequate treatment to reports that represent the kinds the students will encounter on the job.

5

Teaching Aids

C. E. Zoerner, Jr.

Cassette Feedback

Have you ever seen your students disregard your handwritten comments on their papers, glance at their grades, and toss the papers in the nearest wastebasket? Do you mourn the hours of your life so casually discarded?

If so, you may want to try "cassette feedback," a simple technique to multiply your effectiveness as a Business Communications instructor.

From the instructor's point of view, there are powerful advantages in taping comments and criticisms to student papers and then returning the tapes to the students along with their papers. The instructor makes effective use of evaluation time.

The instructor can explain suggestions in detail; point out directions for revision; stop worrying about the wasted red, curt, and perhaps unintelligible marginal comments. The instructor can extend his or her teaching time in an almost tutorial fashion to students who have formed a part of his or her vast anonymous audience.

But what about the student's point of view? How does it feel to be listening to a cassette rather than reading the instructor's comments?

The following findings are based on a casual sample of 100 students who were among the 526 students who received cassette feedback on research papers over the past three years.

1. All but two could demonstrate that they had listened to their tapes. Of the 98 who listened, 41 reported that they did so

initially out of curiosity. (One reported that after 4 months, his curiosity got the best of him.)

2. Eighty-four stated that it was the most useful feedback they had ever received on a finished paper. They felt that their future research papers would be improved as a result of this feedback. Twelve students reported listening to the tapes more than once.

3. Sixty-eight commented that they felt the instruction to be highly "personal," directed to their exact needs.

4. Nine commented that listening to the tape was the first time they could fully believe that their instructor had actually read their paper.

5. Eighty-one students reported that they had learned something from listening to the tape that was in addition to what they had learned by doing the research, preparing the reports, or attending class.

Doris D. Engerrand

Video Tape in the Business Communication Classroom

Students learn more through role-playing and seeing themselves on video tape than through conventional classroom procedures. They select their groups, and each group is taped twice. After the first taping, the group and the class discuss ways in which the situation could be improved—interviewing, for example. The group incorporates the suggestions into the second taping. Both tapes are compared and additional discussion held. Through the use of video tape, students improve oral skills, learn human relations skills, and recognize many communication barriers.

Recently, the Business Department purchased new video tape equipment. Naturally, I wanted to use the equipment to the best advantage for the student; but, after examining the literature and not finding very much on its use in business communication classes, I decided to experiment.

THE ASSIGNMENT

Since my classes are large, normal range thirty to fifty students, in order to get the most out of the time available, I decided that role playing may be the answer. I divided the class into four groups; each group was to act out one of the following situations: disciplining an employee, handling a customer complaint, firing an employee, and interviewing a prospective employee, or interviewing an employee who had left the company. Each student was given the opportunity to select the group of his or her preference, and assignments were made accordingly. The students were instructed to research the literature and to prepare their own five to ten minute skits giving each student a role to play.

Before the first taping, I spent ten to fifteen minutes of one class period (fifty minutes long) scanning the class allowing each member to see and hear himself or herself on television. The purpose of this procedure is to help the students get over the initial shock of seeing themselves as others see them, then hopefully, when the tape is played, they will be more interested in observing the situation as a whole than in seeing themselves. This technique helped, but it did not completely eliminate the problem. I decided not to discuss the four topic areas before taping but to let the situations as the students portrayed them be the starting point. However, the class was instructed to concentrate on the situation and how it was handled.

TAPING SESSIONS

The first group to be taped (disciplining) appeared somewhat apprehensive at first, but they soon ignored the camera and became absorbed in the situation. The taping lasted eight minutes. Immediately after the taping sessions, the members of the group and the class evaluated the performance, pointing out the good as well as the bad points. It is interesting to note that the members of the group concentrated on individual errors (language, appearance, and body movements) while the class concentrated on how people react in disciplining situations. Suggestions were made by the class concerning ways the case could be improved.

I then played the tape, stopping it at various times to reemphasize the points brought out during the initial discussion. After the tape was played, additional comments were made by the group as well as by the class.

A few days later, the same group did the skit again, but taking into consideration the points that had been made during the discussion period. After taping, a discussion was held comparing the two performances. The discussion centered around how the handling of the discipline case was improved and if there should be any more changes. Both tapes were then played, and again I stopped them at critical places to emphasize the points brought out in discussion. After the viewing, the class was given the opportunity to make additional comments. The same procedure was followed for the other groups, handling a customer complaint, firing an employee, and interviewing.

RESULTS OF THE EXPERIMENT

The results of this experiment have been outstanding, in my opinion. Students saw themselves making oral mistakes in the language they were not aware of such as emphasizing the wrong syllable and slurring word endings. The evidence through testing and through student evaluation indicates that the students have not only improved their oral skills, but they have also learned more about the four areas, disciplining, handling complaints, firing, and interviewing than they ever did under regular classroom discussion. In addition, as a bonus, they also learned a great deal about communication barriers.

They learned how various types of behavior in different settings may affect the outcome of the encounter. A few of the barriers the students were able to recognize in the areas of human relations, listening, and speaking were as follows: ignoring the feelings of the listener, being prejudiced acting inconsistently with one's promises, blaming others for misunderstandings, using jargon, responding before thinking, and knowing in advance that one will not believe what the speaker says. Physical barriers recognized were distractions and placement of furniture.

The students have been very enthusiastic. They have learned more through role-playing and seeing themselves on video tape than through the conventional classroom techniques of lecture, discussion, and reports, In my opinion, the use of video tape is a valuable aid in the business communication classroom.

Richard A. Hatch

Using Video Tape to Teach Report Presentation

The intensive feedback provided by videotaping can allow students clearer perceptions of their oral communication performances. Even a short series of experiences with videotape feedback can significantly help students polish their skills. Input from the instructor can be minimal if sessions are carefully planned.

Students in the senior-level Report Writing course at Western Michigan University have previously taken a required speech course, and they have had several experiences in public speaking in other courses. Through these experiences, most of the students have developed a fair level of skill with the basics of public speaking. As a result, the orientation of our instruction in report presentation is to polish fairly competent speakers rather than to eliminat the tics and stutters of the beginner.

For this instruction, groups of six students are asked to meet in the videotape lab for three two-hour sessions outside class. Sessions are organized (in accordance with current theories of micro-teaching) as follows:

1. The learning goals of the sessions are presented, discussed, and (if possible) exemplified.

2. Each student performs for two minutes or so before the camera, attempting to meet the goals of the sessions.

3. The tape is played back. Following each student's playback, he or she is invited to critique his or her performance, commenting both on good and bad points. Other students and

instructor may comment on the critique, but the student's own perceptions of the performance are accepted as the valid ones for purposes of self-improvement.

4. The students are asked to make a formal commitment to themselves, in writing, about specific points they will try to improve during their second performance in the sessions. The students are advised to concentrate upon two or three specific improvements.

5. Each student performs again before the camera, either saying the same thing said the first time or saying another similar thing.

6. The tape is played back again. Each student briefly critiques his or her performance, mentioning the points he or she was concentrating upon or not, as he or she wishes.

Session goals and activities for the three sessions during the most recent semester were these:

Session One: The goal was to polish the students' posture, gestures, and facial expressions—to polish their body language. Students were asked to simply introduce themselves in the first performance and to present a short informal talk on the subject of their choice in the second. They were not asked to prepare either performance beyond simply thinking about what they would say. The tape was played back with sound and again without sound (to accent the body language) after each performance.

Session Two: The goal was to polish the students' ability to respond to unexpected questions. Each student was asked to write five or six topics on slips of paper which were tossed into a hat. Each then drew a slip and immediately responded in a two-minute talk. (If they just couldn't respond to their topic, they were allowed to draw another.) Critiques centered on the coherence of the response.

Session Three: The goal was to polish the students' ability to deliver a short business-type presentation. Students were asked to prepare and deliver a three-minute business-style presentation persuading an audience to do something. Notes on one side of a three-by-five card were allowed. Critiques centered on the structure of the talk and on note-using techniques.

Watching oneself on videotape, it turns out, is such a spur to learning that grading in these sessions has been quite unnecessary. Students are required to attend the sessions as a condition of completion of the course, but they are not graded.

On the basis of several semesters' experience with videotaping, I would suggest that videotape not be used unless the students have the opportunity to spend several sessions observing themselves. Almost universally, the first look at oneself on videotape is pretty depressing, and so a single videotaping can do more harm than good. After the first time or two, however, videotape offers an unparalleled opportunity for a student to take a really objective look at how he or she performs in pubic. Students are really enthused about the results.

Kitty Locker

Teaching with Transparencies

Students in business communication courses need to see both good and bad examples of various kinds of letters and memos. Transparencies offer a useful and versatile means of reproducing examples. They make it easy to discuss visual impact; they allow the instructor to highlight key points and make revisions; they are less likely to produce conscious or unconscious copying than are dittoed or mimeographed examples. This article provides examples to use in teaching You-Attitude and Postitive Emphasis; Format; Subject Lines, Clarity, and Closings; Emotional Appeal in Fund-Raising Letters; Humor in Negative Messages; and Job Applications. A brief discussion of the details which contribute to the success, the partial success, or the failure of each piece of writing is also included. Copies of the examples on a full-size set of transparencies may be obtained from ABCA.

One of the biggest practical problems facing instructors preparing to teach business communication for the first time is finding effective examples. Textbooks have a limited number of examples; one's own mail is likely to yield primarily sales and fund-raising letters. The ideal solution is access to a departmental file of examples gathered over a period of time.

Fran Weeks and his staff at the University of Illinois have compiled an enviable file of examples on permanently-mounted transparencies. These transparencies were an enormous help to me when I began teaching business writing. In the past three years I've accumulated a moderately extensive collection of my own. I'd like to suggest some of the advantages of using transparencies and share some of my favorites—ones which might be useful to teachers looking for examples to use in their own classes. (These examples may be reproduced for classroom use. Publication rights are reserved.)

WHY TRANSPARENCIES?

There are several advantages in putting the examples you use on transparencies rather than duplicating them by ditto or mimeograph. Because transparencies reproduce the original letterhead, type face, and spacing, they make it easy to discuss visual impact. Making a transparency is much faster than typing a stencil. In the classroom, a dozen examples on transparencies are easier to handle than a dozen stacks of handouts. Transparencies provide a more versatile teaching tool. Washable marking pens allow you to highlight key words, point out organization, and even revise. Your comments may be more likely to sink in since your students will be able to see your analysis on the projected image.

Although the initial cost of making a transparency is higher than that of cutting a stencil, transparencies will probably be cheaper than reproducing examples on paper if you use an example for three or four sections or for several semesters. Mounted transparencies are convenient to use, but inexpensive "disposable" transparencies seem reasonably durable: mine show no wear at all after six semesters of use.

Transparencies really prove their worth if you like to show your students examples of good as well as bad writing. Students sometimes find that their creativity is inhibited by good examples in textbooks or handouts; in extreme cases, good examples taken home by students in one section may be plagiarized by students in another. Transparencies are much less likely to produce conscious or unconscious copying.

CHOOSING EXAMPLES

I'm convinced that students need to see both good and bad examples. From a pedagogic point of view, partially successful letters and memos may be the most useful. They enable you to point out that knowing what one ought to do in a letter or memo is of limited value if the writer can't execute his or her plans effectively; they enable you to teach the art of revision. Students can revise an example orally rather quickly, particularly if the errors are glaring ones in tone, organization, or the like; writing a memo from scratch takes considerably more time and may not make the particular point you're trying to cover that day.

Good examples can be taken from both real-world letters and memos and from student papers. The former show students that excellence exists and is valued outside academia; the latter demonstrate that they too can achieve it.

Really bad examples should be used sparingly. They are most useful in helping students avoid major errors. I find that my students' resumes and job applications, particularly, are much better now that we discuss a few disastrous examples and analyze why they fail before the students go off to write their own papers.

USING TRANSPARENCIES

Class discussions of transparencies are likely to be more successful if you read the transparency aloud rather than asking a student to do so or merely waiting while the class reads it silently. To open the discussion, I like to ask my students to identify good and bad elements of the letter or memo, to explain why those elements are good or bad, and to suggest ways the latter could be improved. Such open-ended questions occasionally produce embarrassing results when a student singles out a grievous flaw for praise, but I do think it important that the teacher not prejudge the examples. Students will never be able to revise their own work unless they can tell good points from bad.

When the success or failure of a letter or memo is obvious, it is useful to ask your students what makes it good or bad. If students go beyond their initial impression to analyze the components which produce that effect, they are more likely to retain something they can use in their own writing. In some classes, students will be sufficiently alert to recall the tools of analysis you've given them; in others, you may need to direct their attention specifically to you-attitude, organization, tone, closing, or whatever elements illustrate the point you wish to make that day.

How much time to spend on an individual transparency will vary with your purposes on any given day. Several times during the semester it is worth taking the time to analyze and revise complete paragraphs thoroughly—a process which will take at least fifteen minutes a paragraph even if you lecture. To treat every example in such detail would take an inordinate amount of class time and bore even the most dedicated students. I usually make only two or three main points with one example, neglecting the fine points completely unless a student asks about them. This level of analysis is obviously incomplete, but it enables me to get through considerably more in a class period. If you encourage your students to work inductively, it will be easier to make a point by allowing them to compare and contrast several examples than by examining only one. When students see several ways to approach a given situation, they are also more likely to realize that the examples are only examples, not models to be followed slavishly.

The examples which follow are grouped according to the specific point each most strikingly illustrates. The discussions are far from exhaustive; rather they focus on the details which contribute to the success, the partial success, or the failure of each piece of writing.

YOU-ATTITUDE AND POSITIVE EMPHASIS

The text you assign probably has examples of sentences revised for you-attitude and positive emphasis. I think it's useful to show students additional examples. Transparencies enable you to cover up the "correct" version so that students can revise the originals themselves.

The you-attitude examples in (1) are my own and are designed to illustrate ways of implementing the general principles, "Look at things from your readers' point of view; tell them what they need and want to know; emphasize benefits to them."

—The mere presence of reader benefits does not create you-attitude, for phrasing benefits in terms of what you do for the reader emphasizes how wonderful you are. Instead, focus on how the benefits affect the reader.

—Avoid telling your readers what their emotions are: they may disagree with your diagnosis. Instead, use specifics to describe how they'll benefit.

—Take the sting out of potentially arbitrary demands by showing the reader the justification behind them—preferably one which benefits the reader.

—Merely using the word "you" does not create you-attitude. To employ you-attitude in negative situations, avoid placing blame on the reader. Instead, use passive or impersonal constructions which omit the word "you."

NOT YOU-ATTITUDE	YOU-ATTITUDE
We are happy to grant your application for credit.	Now you may charge your purchases at any Bergner's store.
You will be happy to hear that our walk-up window is now open from 7 till midnight seven days a week.	You can now take care of all your banking needs any day of the week from 7 till midnight at our walk-up window.
We have hired a customer-relations agent.	Our customer-relations agent can answer your questions. Just call this toll-free number . . . .
Send us two copies of your manuscript.	Send us two copies of your manuscript to enable us to reach a decision on it quickly.
You forgot to consider inflation in your estimate.	The estimate makes no allowance for inflation. This factor must be taken into consideration to achieve a reliable figure.

†††

SITUATION	SENTENCE EMPHASIZING POSITIVE ASPECT
You are putting your floor samples and demonstrators on sale. These machines have been in use several hours a day for the past year.	All floor samples and demonstrator machines are on sale, so you get great savings on machines that have already demonstrated their durability and quality in the store.
Your models haven't sold well this year, and as a result, you have more cars to get rid of in your end-of-season clearance sale than do your competitors.	While other dealers can offer you only leftovers, Datsun still has a full line of all our best-selling cars for you to choose from.
The bottle is half empty.	The bottle is half full.

†††

(1)

The first two statements in (1) emphasizing the positive were taken from newspaper ads; I worked backward to arrive at the situation. These examples help to show students that positive emphasis is a matter of viewpoint, not merely of verbal gymnastics. They also illustrate skillful use of connotation to shape the reader's response. The last statement is universally known and helps convince students that positive emphasis is neither difficult nor confined to business communication.

FORMAT

Example (2) is an effective antidote to student complaints that our requirements that every letter or memo be presented in proper format are "mickey mouse." I first used (2) last winter, which in Illinois as in much of the nation was very cold and snowy. My students knew that I was doing consulting work for a Decatur

Hazardous driving conditions have worsened in the Decatur area. Supervisors of salaried employees who face potential problems in returning home should allow those people to leave work with adequate time for safe travel. Latest weather reports indicate up to 14 inches of snow by tonight in the central Illinois area and all roads are hazardous and slippery. South of Decatur, some freezing rain has been reported, and we have received reports that Route 36 east is open to only one lane of traffic. There are no road closings at this time.

It is our intention to be open tomorrow. Any employees who can make it to work should do so. In the event of a change in our plans, we will notify the Decatur news media. Employees are urged to listen to the radio and check their newspapers.

(2)

firm, and when I asked them when they thought the announcement was written, they assumed it had appeared a week or two earlier after an especially heavy snow storm. In fact (although I had been given a copy of this announcement only a short time before), it had been distributed several years earlier. Lacking date or authorship, it permits snow days in perpetuity.

SUBJECT LINES, CLARITY, AND CLOSINGS

Put example (3) up on a screen; then put up (4) and ask students to compare and contrast the two. Observant students will note that these two memos (written by the same author to the same audience, one day apart) have the same subject line. Neither subject line is specific enough to be accurate; the duplication will suggest to recipients that they have two copies of the same memo, and they're likely to throw one away. Moral: subject lines must be specific enough to differentiate any given memo from others on the same general subject.

Example (3) also illustrates how an execrable style can obscure a simple message. The memo responds to the question, will employees be reimbursed for the cost of lunch at conferences they must attend? The answer is no, if the conference is held in the town where the employee's office is; yes, if it's in another town. (The author can't say "where you work" because these employees perform inspections in large geographical areas. The phrase "headquarter city or duty station" is a cumbersome attempt to be accurate.) The style is so impenetrable that few readers will be able to extract any meaning from the memo. Shorter sentences and headings would help.

It will be obvious to your students that the cliché "please don't hesitate to contact" should be revised. Examples (3) and (4) demonstrate that "please call me at . . ." isn't much better. In (3), a conference either is in the same city where an employee's office is or in a different city; there is no middle ground and therefore no reason to expect questions if the policy is explained clearly in the first place. Inviting questions will suggest to some readers that the matter must be more complicated than it appears on the surface.

In (4), the phrases "Essentially I think" and "necessarily" imply that the general statements these phrases modify do not apply to all cases. Having no idea whether or not their cases are

STATE OF ILLINOIS

INTER-OFFICE CORRESPONDENCE

DATE: July 6, 19

MEMO TO: DIVISION MANAGERS AND SECTION MANAGERS OF DIVISION

FROM:

SUBJECT: ATTENDANCE AT CONFERENCES

Travel regulations require that when a meal is included in the conference fee that the request for reimbursement submitted must be reduced by the meal allowance provided for in the travel regulations. For example, if the fee includes a luncheon that fee must be reduced by the $2.00 luncheon allowance. If the conference is held in a location other than the employee's headquarter city or headquarter duty station, the employee may claim the allowance on a travel voucher. However, if the conference location is in the same city as the employee's headquarters or within the same duty station, the employee will not be allowed to charge the luncheon allowance. He would be allowed to charge the evening meal allowance if the conference fee includes a banquet for an evening meal.

If you have any question, please don't hesitate to contact me. Area code 217-525-5620.

RECEIVED

JUL 12 19

EVERY INTER-OFFICE LETTER SHOULD HAVE ONLY ONE SUBJECT.

NOTES

(3)

exceptions, readers are encouraged to call to find out. I tell my students that inviting questions is a good strategy only when a policy has so many provisions and exceptions that listing all of them would be confusing and cumbersome. Otherwise, encouraging the reader to request clarification encourages the writer to be vague or imprecise and negates one of the purposes of writing a memo: to save time needed to make individual explanations.

STATE OF ILLINOIS

INTER-OFFICE CORRESPONDENCE

DATE: July 7, 19

MEMO TO: Division Managers and Section Managers of Division

FROM: [handwritten initials]

SUBJECT: ATTENDANCE AT CONFERENCES

This agency has recently been notified by the Department of Finance that effective immediately all requests for reimbursement of expenses incurred in attending a conference whether in the State of Illinois or outside must be accompanied by a justification of the attendance. Essentially I think this requirement may be fulfilled if the Division or the Section holding the conference would prepare a short statement of justification to be attached to each reimbursement request submitted by the person attending the conference. The justification does not necessarily have to be signed by the employee.

If you have any questions on this matter, please don't hesitate to contact me. Area code 217-525-5620.

RECEIVED

JUL 12 19

EVERY INTER-OFFICE LETTER SHOULD HAVE ONLY ONE SUBJECT.

NOTES

(4)

EMOTIONAL APPEAL IN FUND-RAISING LETTERS

Examples (5) and (6) offer an interesting test of the efficacy of different intensities of emotional appeal in fund-raising letters. After establishing the fact that both letters appeal to the same emotion—compassion for those less fortunate than oneself—I ask my students which letter is more effective. Most students find

THE SALVATION ARMY
Traditional Christmas Appeal

Andrew S. Miller, Lt. Colonel
Unified Commander
Northern Illinois and Chicago
Unified Command

Albin R. Anderson, Chairman
Christmas Committee

The last few days . . .

. . . have been alive with happiness and joy for young and old alike. The Holiday Season has been filled with sounds of laughter and merriment, and we trust you and your family have been a part of it.

But this has not been possible for many less fortunate even though the Salvation Army has been active this Christmas Season. As far as has been humanly and financially possible, The Salvation Army has continued to bring happiness and love and hope to people in your community.

Although we brought the Christmas spirit to more people this year than ever before, it has been done with increased costs for every item used. Need has no season and want and human suffering continue to surround us every day, all year long.

As a supporter of The Salvation Army we are sure that you know Christmas to be a season of giving. Right now your gift is needed to help The Salvation Army meet its financial obligations resulting from a very active Christmas Cheer Program. Your support now has already been translated into moments of happiness and joy and will continue to bring such results in the days to come.

Thank you for your interest, and may God abundantly bless you in the coming year.

Sincerely yours,

Andrew S. Miller, Lt. Colonel
UNIFIED COMMANDER

P.S. If you have already contributed, please accept our thanks and forgive the mailing of the reminder. Thank you.

A.S.M.

(5)

(6) more compelling, but every semester I have a few students who find the strong appeal in (6) offensive. This disparity makes an excellent introduction to a discussion of the advantages and disadvantages of strong emotional appeals in fund-raising letters. On the one had, a mild appeal is unlikely to sway any reader who is not already committed; on the other, readers will reject completely messages whose appeal they find too strong. When

the level of emotional appeal exceeds a reader's personal tolerance, he or she is likely to class the letter as "manipulative" and throw it away. The most practical advice to give students, I feel, is that in their own letters they should not use an emotional appeal which makes them uncomfortable. While a thorough audience analysis can help a writer decide what kind of appeal

THE SALVATION ARMY
Traditional Christmas Appeal

Andrew S. Miller, Lt. Colonel
Unified Commander
Northern Illinois and Chicago
Unified Command

Albin R. Anderson, Chairman
Christmas Committee

Christmas, 19

Mr. Paul J. Larson

Chicago, Illinois 60625

Dear Mr. Larson:

When Patty looked up and said, "Gee, I wish you were my Daddy" -- our caseworker got a lump in his throat and nearly cried.

Patty is five and Billy is six. Their Dad will not be coming home this Christmas. . .any Christmas. There are two other younger children and a lot of love, hope and care in this fine family. Mother works, but is able to provide only a meager existence.

When we talked to the children about Christmas, their eyes sparkled. But on Christmas morning, this sparkle may turn to tears. Unless you help. Need has no season, but at Christmas, The Salvation Army -- with your help again -- tries particularly hard to take families like these into its heart.

Our caseworker's report and a photo of one needy family are enclosed. $39.75 will help turn Christmas from sadness to joy for them. They're typical of the many who urgently need our assistance. $2 will buy a toy. $5 to $15 will buy clothing or food. But $50 or $100 will help more families over a much longer period.

Please share the strength of your love with others this Christmas Season. Give as generously as you can. And while you're enjoying God's bountiful blessings, imagine that some disadvantaged child in this city is saying to you, "Gee, I wish you were my Mommy or Daddy."

May God Bless You,

Albin R. Anderson

P.S. Christmas means so much, especially to children. Please help bring the joy of Christmas into the lives of others, Mr. Larson.

(6)

and what intensity to use, in any mass mailing some readers are likely to find the appeal too strong and others too weak.

It is a useful exercise for students to identify and evaluate the words and details which contribute to the degree of intensity in each letter. Ironically, while the specific case with which (6) opens is effective, the details in paragraph four (designed to convince the reader that this is a real rather than a fictional family) frequently backfire because the specific figure "$39.75" distracts readers. In later versions of this letter, the figure has been rounded off to "$40."

There are other points you can make as well. Letter (6) makes it clear that the money solicited is for the "deserving" poor. Both letters implicitly ask readers to contrast the generous sums they will spend on their own families' Christmas with the comparatively modest donation requested by the Salvation Army. The postscripts are also of interest. That of (6) is adequate but unimpressive; the apology in (5) leaves the reader on a negative note and is particularly ineffective as a deliberate postscript designed to catch the reader's eye before he reads the whole letter.

HUMOR IN NEGATIVE MESSAGES

Humor is not an attribute that most people associate with negative messages. Letters (7) and (8) provide a welcome break from the tedium induced by numerous examples of straightforward negative messages and remind students that creativity has a place in business writing. Like more traditional letters, both (7) and (8) provide buffers, bury the negative request for payment, and end on a success-conscious note. But their real interest lies in their use of humor to forestall the reader's possible negative reaction. In my opinion, example (7) is the more successful of the two.

Although the quote with which (7) opens is on a negative subject, it is rendered neutral both by the impersonality of a law which applies equally to all and by the remoteness in time of Hammurabi's reign. Its subject is exactly that of the letter itself—the circumstances under which a creditor cannot demand repayment of a debt—and facilitates a smooth transitional buffer which stresses the writer's reasonableness. The letter's emphasis on the circumstances under which the reader would *not* owe $6 enables *Intellectual Digest* to subordinate the negative fact that payment is due or past due. (A friend gave me this example; I don't know what stage in the collection process it represented.)

The real source of humor in letter (7) is its challenge to the reader in paragraph two. I suspect that some readers would respond to the letter with documentation of flooding; others might write that drought, not floods, had devasted their crop

Portland Place
Boulder, Colorado 80302

> "If a man owe a debt and Adad innundate his field and carry away produce, or, through lack of water, grain have not grown in the field, in that year he shall not have to make any return of grain to the creditor. . ."
>
> Prologue to
> The Code of Hammurabi
> King of Babylon

Dear Subscriber:

What was good enough for Hammurabi is good enough for INTELLECTUAL DIGEST:

> If you can submit documented evidence that Adad, the storm god, hath inundated your field and carried away produce, I.D. will, under the provisions of The Code of Hammurabi, forgive the $6 our records say you owe us.

I can think of only two other circumstances which might also persuade us to hold off billing:

(1) You already paid, and somehow it hasn't registered with us.

(2) You haven't been receiving I.D.

If any of the circumstances I've noted apply, please let us know promptly. Otherwise, please send us your check so that we can keep sending you I.D.

Sincerely,

Mark V. Earley

Mark V. Earley
Circulation Director

MVE:abc

P.S. While you're at it, why not take advantage of this limited-time offer and extend your subscription: Send us $12 for 2 years or $18 for 3 years.

(7)

and ask if that were covered in Hammurabi's Code. If the magazine is willing to live up to its bargain, such interchanges of wit should be enjoyable for all concerned.

Some students will object that letter (7) is "corny." I would argue that "corniness" is a fault only when the reader feels that it insults his or her intelligence. Letter (7) endeavors to prevent

NEW PROCESS COMPANY
WARREN, PENNSYLVANIA

Dear Customer:

The paper clip coming to you with this letter wasn't dropped in carelessly. He's George -- our office mascot. Please handle him carefully!

The purpose of an ordinary paper clip, as everyone knows, is to hold papers together. But not content with that only, George has accepted complete responsibility for an important mission, which involves:

1. Reminding you NOT TO FORGET to pay NOW for the merchandise shipped you 30 days ago, and for which you were to pay 7 days after receipt.

2. Holding your check and the statement below together throughout his return trip, and

3. Binding, by so doing, the friendly relationship which exists between us.

Won't you please send George back <u>promptly</u> with your payment?

Cordially yours,

NEW PROCESS COMPANY

(8)

that reaction: the logic is tightly structured, and the allusion to Hammurabi flatters readers who recognize the name. (One does not need to be an intellectual to do so; grade children learn about The Code of Hammurabi. The aptness of the citation robs the example of any hint of condescension.)

In (7), humor is an organic part of the message. In (8) it appears "tacked on," and the letter is less successful as a result. Letter (8) comes complete with a real paper clip. The opening paragraphs are clever but contrived: I can't believe that the company really makes paper clips mascots, or names them individually, or that it would send *the* mascot (singular) to a nameless customer. This artificiality might still work if point one were revised. Its legal tone, implying the reader's culpability, contrasts sharply with the notion that the company and the customer are "friends." One simply doesn't ask one's friends to pay one back in that accusatory tone.

Since readers' senses of humor differ, the real test of a collection letter using humor should be, will it enrage readers who think they have paid the bill? Letter (7) passes this test by explicitly acknowledging that the customer's payment may not have "registered with us." Letter (8) however, is likely to antagonize readers who feel they did not forget.

JOB APPLICATIONS

I supplement lectures on application letters with numerous examples. Some of the examples illustrate what I mean by "being specific"; others are designed to prevent an over-literal interpretation of the guidelines I give. (Standard advice, for example, is "Show the reader that you know what the job involves" and "Don't overuse the word 'I'." But I once had a student whose letter started off with six paragraphs of [exceedingly obvious] job description. In the next to the last paragraph the applicant finally mentioned herself; in the last, she implied [not stated] that she was applying for a job. As I now tell my students, that is *not* what that advice means!) After one or two semesters of experience with business communication, you'll have your own favorite examples. New teachers may find (9) and (10) both usable. Both are prospecting letters.

Confident, qualified students may produce arrogant letters inadvertently if they're not careful. I ask my students to examine

November 11, 19

Dear Mr. Smith:

Because your firm has been expanding rapidly, you will be in need of people for internal control. This is where I can help you. I want a job with your company as an internal auditor. I have had the experience of working on the audit staff of a CPA firm during the past two summers and have taken many courses in auditing during college.

Being a staff employee for a CPA firm has given me a practical understanding of internal control. My jobs included confirming receivables and observing inventory. I also developed a cash control system for a large department store and learned how to keep accurate records and the importance of communicating with fellow workers.

While maintaining a "B" average at the University of Illinois, I took many courses in accounting. These courses have given me a thorough background in auditing and have increased my confidence in my ability to help your corporation. I have found that I can adapt to different business situations because my courses have stressed this.

With a young and expanding firm like yours, I see a good chance for promotion for a person of my ability. I would like to talk to you in person about how my experience and education would benefit your firm. Please call me for an interview.

(9)

(9) in some detail to identify the sources of offensive tone and to suggest possible solutions. Students who aren't in accounting may not know what "internal" control is and therefore may not realize the disastrous implication of the first sentence: "Since you're growing so fast, you're undoubtedly hiring a lot of unreliable people who are trying to steal you blind." "I want a job" is much too abrupt.

In the second paragraph, the student fails to capitalize on his strong point. He downgrades the cash control system he developed by attributing one very mundane sentence to it. Instead, he should be more specific. What were the system's features? What problems was it designed to solve? Did it save the store money? Did employees respond more positively to his system than they had to previous systems?

Paragraph three has a number of errors. The subordinate clause is logically (though not grammatically) misplaced; it says, "Even though I got lousy grades in accounting, I still kept a 'B' overall"—hardly the meaning the writer intended to convey. The reader is unlikely to believe that the writer's background is "thorough"; specifics might be more convincing. The last sentence in the paragraph is illogical. It does not follow that one *can* adapt to different situations merely because one's courses have stressed the desirability of doing so. The writer may mean that his knowledge of different accounting methods and auditing techniques will enable him to adapt; his success in handling the simulated cases he has audited in class may indeed indicate that he adjusts easily. Again, specifics would be both more convincing and more logical.

The final paragraph concludes the fiasco with a total lack of you-attitude. (Yes, a student really did write this letter, and no, he didn't know how bad it was.)

Example (10) also exhibits a lack of you-attitude and several logical lapses. (For example, as an undergraduate this paragon has mastered "all facets of insurance theory." One wonders why graduate courses and company training programs exist.) I use (10) because it makes three separate points about name-dropping:

—Use the name of an employee or officer in the company *only* if he or she suggested that you apply. Advising you on the choice of a major is not a sign of special interest; only the most surly adults will refuse to give students casual advice.

—If you have "studied under" someone the reader knows and respects, use the professor's name only if you've gotten more than an "opportunity to learn" from the experience. Prove that you *have* learned by applying facts or theories to the situation of the firm to which you're writing. A term paper or special project may be signs of your achievement; either will need details to be interesting.

—Never refer to relatives in an application letter.

Name-dropping is effective when these guidelines are observed.

November 12, 19__

Allstate Insurance Company
Allstate Plaza
Northbrook, Illinois 60062

Dear Mr. Johnson:

I will be a May, 19__ graduate from the University of Illinois. On the recommendation of the former chairman of the board of your company, George Powell, I specified my studies in finance, majoring in insurance.

Studying under Dr. Robert I. Mehr at the University of Illinois has given me the opportunity to learn under one of the foremost insurance scholars in the United States. I have been taught all facets of insurance theory, with particular emphasis on life insurance and the untapped area of employee benefit plans.

I would be very interested in being considered for employment with Allstate. Your firm is one of the premier companies in the trade, and your new emphasis on group insurance, theory and practice, fits well with my academic background. The opportunities my brother, , has received with Allstate after completing your management training program shows how worthwhile such a program could be to me.

I will be located in the Chicago area after June 1, 19__. I would be available for an interview any time after then, and look forward to hearing from you soon.

(10)

A FINAL WORD

A steady diet of transparencies would be as deadly as a steady diet of lectures. By varying transparencies with other activities—discussions, group projects, in-class writing assignments, etc.—you can have lively classes in which your students have fun learning.

[If you would like a full-size set of the transparencies illustrated in this article, send your $10 check to: ABCA, 317-B David Kinley Hall, Urbana, IL 61801, tell us you want "Locker's Transparencies." PREPAID orders only, please.]

Francis W. Weeks

How to Write Problems

When Professor Weeks came to the University of Illinois as a teaching assistant, he was put to work writing and editing problems for the problem manual authored by Alta Gwinn Saunders and C. R. Anderson. He has been involved with successive editions of this problem manual ever since. The latest edition is **Business Writing Cases and Problems: Letters, Memorandums, and Reports,** *by Francis W. Weeks and Richard A. Hatch, published by Stipes Publishing Company, Champaign, Illinois.*

Central to the teaching of business communication is the problem—the daily or weekly application by students of their knowledge and skill to situations that require effective communication. Teachers may lecture all they want to. Students may read the textbook cover to cover and do additional readings in the library. But the real learning takes place when the student has to solve a problem, a communication problem, either by writing something or by making an oral presentation.

Good problems are hard to find. When we do find one, we assign it so often that it wears out quickly. Student papers begin to look strikingly similar to some we have seen before. Then we decide that, since the problem was such a good one, we can change a few things in it and use it over again, but altering the problem is seldom successful. Alterations and revisions are rarely as good as the originals. Something essential seems to be lost while making what appear to be minor changes. Perhaps the best thing to do is to let the problem rest awhile and then revive it. Still, the quest for new, good problems is a constant one.

WHAT MAKES A PROBLEM GOOD?

To put it succinctly, a good problem is one from which the student learns something about communication while developing skill in writing or speaking. The primary purpose is not to test students' knowledge of the textbook, but to enable them to carry their learning beyond books into the realm of application, and, by applying, to learn more. A list of qualities of a good problem would probably include these characteristics:

1. The problem seems real. Note the word "seems." It does not have to *be* real. Sometimes a real problem taken from an actual business situation seems unreal to the students, and they don't believe it. It does little good to tell them that the situation really happened—an illustration of the old adage "truth is stranger than fiction." In writing problems, fiction is fine, if it appears true to life.
2. Students should be able to understand the problem situation without mastery of specialized knowledge. The purpose of the problem is to teach communication not computer science.
3. The problem should be appropriate to the stage of the course when it is assigned and to the expected development of students' skills at that point.
4. There should be enough detail in the problem so that the student can play the assigned role with confidence. Yet there should not be so much detail that students can copy the problem word for word when writing their solutions.
5. The purpose and scope of the problem should be very clear. The students should know what the objective of the communication is so that all will be writing to the same end.
6. It would be nice if the scope of the problem could be explained fully in writing without going into too much detail. But details often have to be left to class discussion which can amplify or modify the written explanation.
7. The "audience" (readers or listeners) should be clearly visualized and described. Students need to know whom they are writing to. Again, class discussion can develop this.
8. The result expected from the communication should be clear. Students should understand what is supposed to happen after the communication is received.
9. The problem should not be too easy. Every problem should present a challenge of some sort to the student, although routine situations are often useful for in-class exercises.

SOURCES OF PROBLEMS

So where do we go to find problems that meet those nine criteria? The first thought is to look at the ends of the chapters of various textbooks, since publishers often require authors to include problems in the books. But many of the problems found there are not adequately explained and would be useful only if expanded and, in effect, rewritten by the teacher. For example: "Pick a product you are familiar with and write a letter selling it by mail." Before writing a sales letter, students have to be led through product analysis, "audience" analysis, listing of selling points, choosing of a central selling point, etc. Left to choose without guidance, students will pick *Playboy* or *Ms.*—without knowing anything about the selling features of the magazines or about the people who might subscribe to them.

The teacher can use his or her own experience with businesses, but in many cases these are experiences with retail business. It's interesting to note that the textbooks of the 1920's dealt almost exclusively with retail stores and their customers. Organizational communication had not yet been systematically studied. Problems often had to do with writing adjustment letters; e.g., answering a complaint to a mail order house because they sent the wrong shoes, or something like that. Our present generation of students may have something to do with retail businesses, but they are more likely to go into large business organizations where they will first write internal memos about organizational problems. If the teacher has worked in a company and become familiar with such problems, then that experience could be a fruitful source of good problem material.

Probably the best source of problems is the experience that many teachers get from conducting training programs, seminars, and short courses for companies or for groups of business executives. A useful exercise in such programs is to require participants to bring examples of their own writing. Getting a good problem from these writing examples is sometimes akin to finding the needle in the haystack, but occasionally one crops up, and the teacher can take it back to class and use it effectively. Sometimes one can enlist the cooperation of people in business in writing problems.

Students themselves are sources of problems. Most of them have worked, part-time or full-time, in businesses during vacations or while in school. As an assignment, ask them to describe a communication problem from their own work experience. Occasionally you get a good problem that way.

COMMON SHORTCOMINGS OF PROBLEMS

The great difficulty in writing a good problem is to make it include everything that is necessary for the student but to still have a short problem. This is the difficulty that textbook authors face. They cannot devote a large number of pages to problems and usually not several pages to one problem. Therefore, they try to write problems so that several, sometimes many, can fit on one page. Yet the problem should include the definition of purpose, some indication of the scope of the problem, some description of the "audience" for the communication, some explanation of the role that the student is expected to play in the situation, plus enough description of the situation so that the student will feel comfortable in writing about it. Doing this in one short paragraph is very difficult and sometimes impossible.

Consequently, the principal shortcoming of the problems that we see is that they do not tell enough. The student has to be imaginative enough to fill in everything that is missing, and some students have great difficulty in doing this. The other answer, as mentioned above, is for the teacher to fill in the picture by means of extensive briefing in class. (And then the night before the assignment is due, the student calls up and says "I don't understand what I'm supposed to do with this problem.")

ARE THERE ANY GOOD SHORT PROBLEMS?

Yes there are some good, short problems, and with luck each teacher finds some. Here is one which originated in the warehouse of a large grocery chain. The warehouse foreman was enrolled in a short course on improving written communications and submitted this memo as an example of his writing. Without any explanation at all, it almost makes a satisfactory problem with the simple instruction to rewrite it:

To: F. E. Jones Date:

From: J. R. Smith

Subject: POWER TRUCKS

Referring to my letter of August 30 concerning the historical data of our power trucks. At the time we reviewed this, the two Acme units were costing more to operate and keep in repair than the three Yale trucks. This trend is still true. It seems that the Acme units have more exposed moving parts and as our operation is extremely wet, we continue to replace bearings and other parts to keep these in an operating condition. I realize the Yale trucks are the oldest, but in my opinion, they seem to operate more economically in our plant than the Acme units. Whatever we should get in the future, it should be well protected so water does not get into the mechanical parts of the machine. It is my considered opinion that we should replace the Acme trucks with Yale trucks. The initial cost is approximately the same and as shown above they operate more economically.

It would appear that a little more instruction than "rewrite" ought to be given to the students; thus, these instructions were added to the problem:

1. The subject line is too vague and general. Pin it down.
2. The opening sentence is incomplete. The "letter" referred to was a memo. "Historical data" refers to the explanation which is given here and was given earlier.
3. The word "trend" is used inaccurately to refer to a situation which has not changed.
4. "It seems that" should not be used to refer to a provable fact.
5. Organize the information in a logical sequence. Make the recommendation stand out by putting it either first or last. Paragraph correctly.

What is missing from the problem is some discussion of who the people are. Most students have not worked as foremen in warehouses. What is it like to be a foreman? Who are the people a foreman communicates with on the job? Who's the boss who will read the memo? Although this problem was used for years at the University of Illinois, these questions were never answered on paper. They were brought up in the class briefing.

The problem worked so well that it was used for years and finally simply wore out—except that it is still useful for in-class writing. There was no way to change it or alter it without ruining it as a problem.

A similar problem came out of the same warehouse and had to do with ripening of bananas. The author thought it was a fine problem. All it involved was answering a simple question: "Can you ripen enough bananas so that we can send some to Chicago in addition to satisfying our local needs?" The student had to do a little elementary figuring, (adding, subtracting, and multiplying) and come up with an "iffy" answer, but the problem never worked successfully. Although the author used it a few times, the students never did "get with it." And other teachers who tried it gave up on it, saying it just wouldn't work. Thus the problem that the teacher may think is a great one sometimes turns out to be a dud. *Moral:* thoroughly test your problems before you put them into a book or commit them to some other form of publication.

CASES MAKE BEST PROBLEMS

Years ago a CPA firm wrote a study of dictation problems in a large agricultural co-op and recommended the installation of a centralized dictation system. This was converted to a problem which, according to Richard Hatch of San Diego State, is "the best problem ever written." Since it was such a good problem, it was used extensively and therefore had to be revised because too many "A" solutions were floating around the campus.

Unfortunately, the problem is too long to reproduce here, but if it were reproduced, it should be in the original version. Every time it was revised something happened to make it less effective. It was very difficult to keep all the internal data consistent through the various revisions, and students were quick to point out the inconsistencies. The latest version of this problem can be found in Weeks and Hatch, *Business Writing Cases and Problems: Letters, Memorandums, and Reports,* and of course it is now a Word Processing Center problem. The next time around the "bugs" should be worked out of it.

Since Word Processing Centers are currently much in vogue, any teacher could write a case study about the installation of a WPC. All the teacher needs is to find a company which has just installed one or is about to, get some facts and figures from the company, get a little help from one of the manufacturers such as Lanier or Norelco, and write a case study.

The advantages of such a case study, despite the length, is that it can spawn a variety of writing situations: e.g., a report, obviously; a summary or abstract of the report; a cover letter; possibly an oral report; etc.

Considering the omnipresence of computers, case studies and problems involving computer installations and use of computers should be "relevant" to the interests of our students. But writing such case studies or problems presents many difficulties, and I have seen only one or two good problems coming out of the world of computer applications.

The ABCA Bulletin tries to help teachers in the area of problem writing and assigning. There's a regular feature called "My Favorite Assignment" and all teachers of business communication are invited to submit contributions to this feature. Since good problems are so hard to come by, it is important that we share the good ones with each other.

ABOUT OUR CONTRIBUTORS

John E. Binnion has earned degrees from Chaffey College in California, The University of Texas at Austin, New Mexico Highlands University, The University of Denver, and Oklahoma State University. His professional credentials include the Certified Public Accountant Certificate and the Certified Administrative Manager Certificate, as well as the Local Preachers License of the Methodist Church. He has been listed in *Who's Who in America* since 1964.

Joel P. Bowman began teaching business communication in 1965 as a graduate teaching assistant at the University of Illinois. After a tour of duty with the Army and completing his Ph.D. in English, Bowman taught business communication and report writing at the University of Florida. In 1975 Bowman moved to Western Michigan University, where he coordinates the business communication program. He is the co-author of *Understanding and Using Communication in Business* (Canfield Press 1977) and *Effective Business Correspondence* (to be released by Canfield Press in 1979). He is currently working on *The Professional Secretary*, a joint authorship textbook for Science Research Associates.

Joseph F. Ceccio received his Ph.D. from the University of Illinois at Urbana-Champaign. Currently, he is Assistant Professor of English at Wright State University in Dayton, Ohio, where he teaches business and professional communication. He has written articles for *The ABCA Bulletin* and reviews for *The Journal of Business Communication*. His textbook *Medicine in Literature* has recently been published by Longman, Inc., New York. He was cochairman of the 1978 ABCA Midwest Regional Conference held in Dayton.

L. W. Denton is assistant professor of English and coordinator of the business and technical writing courses at Auburn University. He has published in *The Journal of Business Communication, Engineering Education, The Harvard Theological Review*, and several other journals. Currently he is doing research on in-house training programs in written communication and participates actively in continuing education by offering short courses to various state government agencies in Alabama.

Mrs. Jean Dickey is completing her 13th year as a teacher in the College of Business at Southeast Missouri State University,

Cape Girardeau, Missouri. A graduate of the University of Tulsa (MBE), she taught high school students prior to her association with the University. In addition to her teaching duties, she busies herself with rose gardening, water sports, church activities, and traveling.

Juanita Williams Dudley is Associate Professor and Director of Technical Writing at Purdue University, West Lafayette, Indiana. She has published numerous articles on technical writing—most notably in *The ABCA Bulletin*, *The Journal of Business Communication*, and *English Education.* Her credentials and experience include: M.F.A., Writer's Workshop, University of Iowa, 1964; editor and science writer for the Menninger Foundation (Topeka, Kansas), 1964-65; lecturer and professor of scientific, technical, and business writing from 1965 through present. In 1977, Mrs. Dudley was awarded an Excellence in Teaching Award by Purdue's School of Humanities, Social Science, and Education. Her current research interest is alternative course structures and innovative teaching methods.

Doris D. Engerrand is Associate Professor and Coordinator of the Department of Business Education and Office Administration at Georgia College, Milledgeville, Georgia. She holds two Bachelor's degrees from North Georgia College and Master's and Ph.D. degrees from Georgia State University. She has received many honors during her teaching career, is a member of four honor associations, and is listed in several biographies. She is currently vice-president of the Southeast Region of ABCA.

Herman A. Estrin is Professor of English at New Jersey Institute of Technology, formerly Newark College of Engineering. He has recently served as the President of the New Jersey Council of Teachers of English and edited an anthology *The Teaching of Technical Writing* (with Donald Cunningham) published by the National Council of Teachers of English.

Ross Figgins, Ph.D., is primarily a professor although he has also been a contractor, draftsman, journalist, author, and communications consultant. He has taught at the Universities of Illinois and Southern California, as well as California State Polytechnic University. His writing interests include both professional and creative efforts, the latter focusing on the Japanese *haiku* form. His books include *Techniques of Job Search* (Harper & Row, 1976), *American Haiku* (Raindrop Press, 1978), and *The Job Game: Playing to Win* (in search of a publisher).

Richard A. Hatch teaches business writing and data processing at San Diego State University. He received the Ph.D. in Communication from the University of Illinois in 1969, and he taught business communication at the University of Illinois (Urbana) and at Western Michigan University. He is author of *Communicating in Business*, published by Science Research Associates.

Jo Ann Hennington is an associate professor in the College of Business Administration at Arizona State University in Tempe, Arizona. She received her doctorate at that university in 1972 and was invited back to teach in the Administrative Services Department of the College of Business in 1975. She is currently serving in an administrative position as Director of Academic Advisement for the College of Business as well as performing classroom teaching assignments.

Pernell Hayes Hewing is Assistant Professor of Business Communication at the University of Wisconsin—Whitewater. She received the Master's degree from Temple University, Philadelphia, Pennsylvania and the Ph.D. degree from the University of Wisconsin—Madison, Madison, Wisconsin. Her professional memberships include: Delta Pi Epsilon, Wisconsin Business Education Association, American Business Communication Association, National Business Education Association, and Milwaukee Business Education Association. Among her honors are: Outstanding Educators of America (1971), *Who's Who Among Women of the World*—published in London (1975), and *Who's Who Among Black Americans* (1976).

Herbert W. Hildebrandt has been at The University of Michigan since 1958 and holds two appointments: Professor of Business Administration and Professor of Speech. His writings include the books: *Public Speaking for College Students; Issues of Our Time;* and books on communication for businesspersons. He has authored over 50 articles on communication. Recently, he was voted an outstanding teacher by university colleagues and received the coveted Amoco Good Teaching Award. He lectures frequently on communication in Europe, particularly in Berlin, Heidelberg, Mainz, London, Brussels, and Vienna.

Arax Hogroian received a B.A. from Hunter College and an M.S. in Business Education from the same institution. She has taught at both Hunter College and Herbert H. Lehman College of the City University of New York. Her favorite subject—Communication; her students—men and women from many phases of business. In addition to teaching, she has served in diverse areas of business and industry with high level corporate executives. As Assistant Director of Public Relations with the American Bankers Association, she developed and managed a comprehensive educational film program (motion pictures coordinated with printed teaching materials) used nationally in community/school relations by the banking industry. Currently, she is a public relations/communications consultant.

Daphne A. Jameson teaches business and technical communication at the University of Illinois, where she is completing a Ph.D. in English. She did undergraduate work in mathematics and English at Ohio State. She has taught college rhetoric and literature courses, as well as secondary school English, journalism, and mathematics.

Margaret MacColl Johnson holds the B.A. degree from Smith College and the M.S. from Simmons College, Boston, Mass. Her practical experience in public relations qualifies her for accreditation from the Public Relations Society of America as a public relations counselor. From 1967-1972 she taught business communication to students of Michigan State University's College of Business (in addition to administrative duties as assistant to the dean of the college). She is currently on both the Continuing Education and Open Division faculties of Roger Williams College, Bristol, R.I., teaching both technical communication and public relations.

Don Leonard received his B.S. and M.B.A. degrees from Nicholls State University in Thibodaux, Louisiana. In 1977, he was awarded a Ph.D. in Management from Louisiana State University in Baton Rouge. In his program, he minored in Marketing and studied Communications as a working area. Since 1974 he has served as Assistant Professor of Business Communications in the Department of Administrative Services at Arizona State University.

Kitty Locker is an Assistant Professor of English at Texas A&M University. She earned her Ph.D. at the University of Illinois, where she learned the craft of Business Communication by teaching in Fran Weeks' program there. She has had several articles published or accepted for publication in *The ABCA Bulletin* and *The Journal of Business Communication.*

W.J. "Jack" Lord, Jr., is Chairman, Department of General Business, The University of Texas at Austin, and Professor of Business Communication. During 27 years' teaching experience, he has authored four books—most recently, *Functional Business Communication*, 2nd ed—numerous manuals, and contributes regularly to professional journals. A Senior Member of the American Business Communication Association, he has served on or chaired numbers of committees, was 1974 ABCA President, and was elected an ABCA Fellow the same year. Recipient of three Teaching Excellence Awards and various other citations of merit, he was John R. Emens Distinguished Professor, Ball State University, Spring 1978.

Karl M. Murphy obtained his A.B. at Kent State University and his Ph.D. at Harvard University. Before entering teaching he was employed by the B.F. Goodrich Company in its Factory Service Division. Almost all his teaching career has been spent at the Georgia Institute of Technology, where he is currently the Head of the English Department. He is the author of numerous articles on professional and general topics, as well as a text, *Modern Business Letters.* For many years he has worked with the American Business Communication Association in various capacities, serving as its President in 1970. He is also active as a writing consultant to government and industry.

Nicholas J. Pasqual teaches technical writing, journalism, composition, and criminal justice communications at Southeastern Community College, West Burlington, Iowa. He learned business communications at the University of Illinois, where he was a teaching assistant in the Division of Business and Technical Writing. He also is a former news reporter (with the *Peoria*, Illinois, *Journal Star*); he holds master's degrees in English as a Second Language and Journalism, from the University of Illinois at Urbana-Champaign.

John N. Penrose holds a B.S.J. and an M.S. in journalism from Ohio University and a Ph.D. in Communication from the University of Texas. In the past 12 years he has taught letter and report writing, organizational communication, management, and marketing courses at Ohio University, Southern Illinois University at Edwardsville, and the University of Texas. He has been a frequent contributor to *The Journal of Business Communication* and *The ABCA Bulletin*, and an active member of the American Business Communication Association. Publications, committee work, and personal interests focus on teaching methodology, the job-getting process, and communication auditing. He is currently teaching business communication at the University of Texas.

Judy Ponthieu has her Ph.D. from Texas Tech and taught Managerial Communication courses for five years at Tech. She is now in Personnel Administration at a Lubbock hospital.

Donald P. Rogers (Ph.D. Ohio, '73) is Assistant Professor, Organizational Communication, and Director of Undergraduate Studies in the Department of Communication, Faculty of Social Sciences and Administration, State University of New York at Buffalo.

Tom Sawyer received his Ph.D. in Speech from the University of Michigan in 1953. Subsequently he was employed part-time as a technical editor and later as a part-time research associate on psychological experiments studying critical flicker fusion and random human behavior. His technical expertise in this field is best revealed in his article, "How To Do An Experiment Involving Electronic Equipment," *Phi Kappa Phi Journal*, Fall 1971. He was a Fulbright Lecturer in Lahore, Pakistan in 1963-64, Chairman of his department in 1966-71, and Visiting Professorial Fellow at the University of Wales Institute of Science and Technology in 1972.

Natalie R. Seigle, a Rhode Island native, is an Instructor in Business Communications, Business Department, Providence College, Providence, R.I. She has a B.S. in Business Administration from Simmons College, an M.A. in English from the University of Rhode Island, and has done graduate study in Linguistics and the English Language at the University of Cambridge, England. She is married, has three children, and one grandchild. Her recent publications include articles in *The Magazine of Bank Administration*, *R.I. Jewish Historical Notes*, and several *ABCA Bulletins*. Mrs. Seigle is listed in *Who's Who in the East*, *Dictionary of International Biography*, and *The World's Who's Who of Women*.

Edward G. Thomas, a native of Kentucky, earned his B.S. and M.A. degrees at Western Kentucky University and his Ed.D. at the University of Kentucky. He joined the Faculty of the James J. Nance College of Business Administration at Cleveland State University in 1973. He is now an Associate Professor of Business Education, Assistant Dean of the College of Business Administration, and Director of Graduate Programs at Cleveland State University. He has published articles in a wide variety of journals, including *The ABCA Bulletin*, *Delta Pi Epsilon Journal*, *Journal of Vocational Behavior*, *NBEA Yearbook*, *Management World*, *Journal of Small Business Management*,

Journal of Business Education, *Business Education Forum*, *Business Education World*, and *The Balance Sheet*. He was selected for listing in the 1977 edition of *Outstanding Young Man of America*.

David P. Throop teaches business and technical communication at the University of Illinois. Originally an engineering student, he received B.A. and M.A. degrees in English from Illinois, where he is currently completing an M.B.A. He has also taught college rhetoric and literature courses.

James T. Watt is Associate Professor of Business Administration at Texas Tech. His Ph.D. is from The Ohio State University. All of his teaching experience is in the area of business communications and includes the "traditional" written communications courses as well as courses in organizational communications. Watt has had ten years of business experience and has served as consultant to several business organizations. He is coauthor of *Communication in Business*.

Francis W. Weeks is professor and director of Business and Technical Writing at the University of Illinois (Urbana); Executive Director of the American Business Communication Association; and an honorary member of the Japan Business English Association. He is author of *Principles of Business Communication* and editor of *Readings in Communication from Fortune;* coauthor of *Business Reports* and *Business Writing Cases and Problems*. As a trainer, educator, and consultant on problems of written communication, Fran has served such major companies as State Farm Insurance, Union Carbide, Caterpillar, Westinghouse Air Brake Company, Litton Industries, Fluor, and A.E. Staley, as well as two major CPA firms: Touche, Ross, and Alexander Grant.

Barron Wells received his Doctorate from the University of Houston in 1971, and his Master's and Bachelor's degrees from Northwestern State University of Louisiana in 1965 and 1960, respectively. He is currently Coordinator of Business Communication at the University of Southwestern Louisiana, where he has taught for the past 5 years. Other teaching experiences include: Indiana State University, Northwestern State University of Louisiana, and Louisiana Public High Schools. He has also contributed several articles to various professional publications. A native of Louisiana, he is married and has 2 children.

Clyde W. Wilkinson—professor, author, and consultant—holds four degrees in three fields from four schools (Weatherford

College, University of Texas, University of Pennsylvania, University of Illinois). A native Texan, he has taught at Texas A&M, Pennsylvania, Illinois, Army University (Florence, Italy), Texas, Michigan State, Florida, and Alabama. He has written numerous journal articles and three books on business communication: *Business Communication Problems* (three editions with C.R. Anderson and F.W. Weeks), *Writing for Business* (three editions with J.H. Menning and C.R. Anderson), and *Communicating Through Letters and Reports* (five editions with J.H. Menning, sixth with Peter B. Clarke). The Seventh Edition, with Clarke and Dorothy C.M. Wilkinson, is in preparation for 1980 publication.

Charlotte A. Williams is Instructor in Management in the Florida State University College of Business. She is in the dissertation stage of a doctoral program in Communication at FSU and holds an M.S. in Higher Education and B.A. in English. Her publications and consulting have been in the areas of organizational communication and information theory. She is a member of Phi Beta Kappa, Beta Gamma Sigma, Phi Kappa Phi, Sigma Tau Delta, Academy of Management, Southern Management Association, and the American Business Communication Association, and is included in *Who's Who of American Women*.

James P. Zappen is Assistant Professor, Department of Humanities, College of Engineering, The University of Michigan, Ann Arbor, Michigan. His B.A. and M.A. are from the University of Detroit, and his Ph.D. (Renaissance Studies) from the University of Missouri at Columbia. Before joining the faculty at Michigan, he was an assistant professor at Western Michigan University where he taught informational and advanced business writing.

C.E. Zoerner, Jr. holds a Ph.D. in Communications from the University of Illinois at Urbana-Champaign. He has taught writing in high schools, junior colleges, colleges, and universities, including the University of Illinois and the University of Southern California. Under his own name he is published widely in the academic and popular press, and recently he finished his second ghost-written book. Presently Chair of the Management/Marketing Department in the School of Management at California State University—Dominguez Hills, he lives in Manhattan Beach, California, with his wife and four children.

you have a professional interest in the communications of business . . .

you are invited to join the American Business Communication Association. Teacher, administrator, or practitioner, you will find ABCA the association for all who are seriously interested in business communication—written, oral, and graphic.

ABCA was founded in 1935 and now has a membership of more than 1100, including professors of world-wide reputation, well-known authors, training directors, business executives, and consultants. Association with such people will allow you the opportunity to keep up with professional research and developments, as well as share your own ideas and work experience.

For example, four times a year you'll receive **The Journal of Business Communication** with its papers on important aspects of business communication and its reviews of major books. You are encouraged to submit articles for consideration.

You'll also receive a second quarterly publication, **The ABCA Bulletin,** which carries course descriptions for senior college, junior college, and high school; company training programs; bibliographies; class problems and solutions; and other useful material.

ABCA's publication program makes a number of other books and pamphlets available: a casebook, a special bulletin on employment, a comprehensive bibliography, and a career booklet (forthcoming).

Finally, regional meetings and the national convention will enable you to meet and talk with leaders in the profession.

To enjoy these opportunities, just ask ABCA for a membership application. When you return it, along with your check for dues, you will be enrolled immediately and receive the current issues of the **Journal** and **Bulletin**. Write to Francis W. Weeks, Executive Director, The American Business Communication Association, 911 South Sixth Street, Champaign, Illinois 61820.

You'll be glad you did. And we'll be glad to meet you.